Janet Leach
A Potter's Life

by Emmanuel Cooper

Janet Leach: A Potter's Life

by Emmanuel Cooper

Assistant Editors: Fiona Sibley and Natasha Cawley
Design and Production: Ben Eldridge
Production Assistant: Yo Thom
Index: Mark Walton

Cover: Janet Leach throwing, 1970s

ISBN-10 0-9523576-8-2
ISBN-13 978-0-9523576-8-1

Published by Ceramic Review Publishing Ltd,
25 Foubert's Place, London W1F 7QF

© 2006 Emmanuel Cooper

Contents

Preface 4

Introduction 6
Tie a Yellow Ribbon

1. Lone Star State..14
Texas 1918-37

2. A Sculptor in New York 18
America 1937-49

3. The Human Being as the Universe 26
Threefold Farm 1949-54

4. Pottery Heaven..38
Japan 1954-55

5. Manager, Wife, Potter 62
St Ives 1956-62

6. A New Beginning 98
St Ives 1962-74

7. The Accidental and the Incidental 112
St Ives 1974-79

8. Innovation and Consolidation 132
St Ives 1979-97

Postscript 142

Selected Exhibitions..144
Chronology 146
Bibliography 148
Footnotes/Collections/Illustrations 151
Acknowledgments 152
Index 153

Preface

This is the third book I have written on leading potters from the Leach family. The first, published in 2003, was a detailed account of the life and work of Bernard Leach (1887-1979),[1] followed by the book on Leach's eldest son David (1911-2004),[2] which coincided with a retrospective of his pots. The present book is on the life and work of Janet Darnell Leach (1918-1997), the third wife of Bernard Leach, who lived in St Ives until her death. All have been written with the help of the Leach family and with full access to the extensive Leach archives held at the Crafts Study Centre. The research has involved many hours of interviews with people central to the stories, as well as access to much privately owned material. The books are intended to give a rounded and full picture of two generations of the Leach family, and their important contribution to twentieth century studio pottery.

Janet Darnell Leach was a gifted potter in her own right who soon established her individual voice at St Ives, although her talents were often seen to be overshadowed by her famous and distinguished husband, Bernard Leach. He was some thirty years older than Janet and there were always questions about the motivations for the marriage; to what extent, for instance, had she married solely for love or as part of a career move in associating herself with one of the world's leading potters? Certainly, with her strong, bony features and black curly hair, she was a strikingly handsome young woman, vivacious, lively and intelligent, who was prepared to argue and debate with Leach about pots. Leach, although much older, was charismatic, charming and distinguished. Almost inevitably there was a clash of personalities that was both personal and artistic.

Fiercely independent, Janet Leach looked for equality within the marriage while Leach sought a relationship that

[1] Emmanuel Cooper, *Bernard Leach: Life and Work*, Yale University Press, London, 2003
[2] Emmanuel Cooper and Kathy Niblett, *David Leach*, Richard Dennis, Somerset, 2003

more conventionally reflected the traditional husband and wife roles. The independence that Janet sought, most significantly, extended to her work as a potter. She had no interest in following Leach's style and, far from admiring the refined stonewares and porcelains of China and Korea from which he drew inspiration, her ideas and stimulation came from the leathery, flame-marked surfaces and asymmetrical pots made in places such as Tamba and Bizen that had their origins in Korean pottery. She found particular enjoyment in the freer, more organic forms. These were not the pots that Leach responded to and he was forever attempting to acknowledge her individuality as an artist while recognising that he did not fully understand her work.

Although Janet Leach's most important inspiration came from her training in Japan, where she was one of the few women to study in a totally male dominated craft, her pots brought together an eclectic range of influences. Born in Texas, she worked as a sculptor in New York before discovering clay and moving to Japan to train in traditional country potteries. Most of her working life was spent as a potter in St Ives, England, where she found her own style. Her pots – with their blend of austerity and sensuality combined with a sense of drama and serenity – are instantly recognisable. This book tells her story, starting with her childhood, her work with the Federal Art Project, her pottery at Threefold Farm in New York State, her two years in Japan and her time in England managing the Leach Pottery. It looks at her often turbulent relationship with Leach and sorts out fact from fiction, myth from reality.

At times Janet Leach could be domineering and forceful, but she could also be kind, responsive and thoughtful, all qualities that are reflected in her pots. As a manager she was attentive to the needs of the potters at St Ives and sought to establish a creative environment, although this was occasionally volatile. As a gifted artist with something to say, she followed her own ideas in her work, seeking a dynamic balance between strength and sensitivity. Her intriguing and often complex story gives insights into the work of one of the most significant potters of the late twentieth century.

Emmanuel Cooper

Introduction
Tie a Yellow Ribbon

ABOVE: Janet Leach, c1985

OPPOSITE: Janet Leach – Cylindrical pot, coiled, thrown and beaten, red stoneware with poured ash-type glaze, c1980, H36cm (Photo: David Westwood; Collection: Crafts Study Centre)

Reminiscing towards the end of her life, Janet Darnell Leach said that when she died, she wanted a yellow ribbon to be tied, not on 'the Old Oak Tree', but on her pots. The yellow ribbon, with no obvious ceramic associations, reflected both her loyalty to Texas – the place of her birth – and to the great melting pot of cultures that is America, for Janet saw herself as part of the diverse ethnic traditions that make up the country. She had no inhibitions about responding to many sorts of influences, whether pots produced by First Nation potters in America or the work of traditional Japanese and Korean potters, while also relating to European concepts of the individual potter. All are sensitively and thoughtfully brought together in her distinctive, strong, bold, sculptural pots that often seem to be hewn out of the earth.

With experience as a sculptor in New York before and after the Second World War, two years' study in country potteries in Japan and most of her working life spent as a potter in England, Janet Leach's life spanned several continents and diverse cultures, all successfully synthesised in forms, many of which seem to have a powerful sense of organic growth. Working always at high temperatures in flame-burning kilns where body and glaze fuse to become one, she investigated variations of established shapes that include rounded or tall bottles, slab-built pots and flat dishes in stoneware and porcelain, finding subtle new meanings within each series of shapes. Variations to the bodies, glazes and firings enabled her to explore different effects and discover new subtleties of expression.

Just as Janet Leach's pots fit no neat style or category, she also resists Michael Cardew's intriguing analysis that divides potters into those attracted by mud and water and those to fire and flame.[1] Although she claimed to have

[1] The title of a film made about Cardew's work was *Mud and Water Man*. Cardew placed himself in the former category

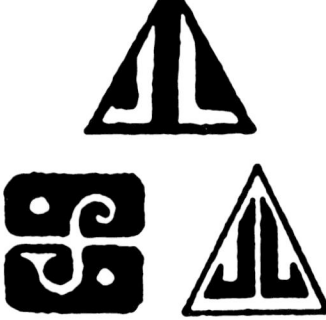

ABOVE TOP: Janet Leach pottery stamp – JL and St Ives

ABOVE BOTTOM: Janet Leach – Pot, coiled and thrown, faceted top, saltglaze, c1960, H about 15cm

[2] Letter to author 1989. n.d.
[3] A general term for the work of abstract expressionists in the US and elsewhere, where the marks on the canvas are thought to be a record of the artist's physical gestures as well as their emotions at the time when the painting was made, often reflecting the influence of calligraphy
[4] When writing approvingly of the work of Lucie Rie, whom she described as a 'kitchen potter', Janet admired the way she succeeded in avoiding such 'masculine concepts' as digging clay and chopping wood. Quoted in Moira Vincentelli, *Women and Ceramics: Gendered Vessels*, Manchester University Press, 2000, p233

'always been a fire potter',[2] Janet was just as concerned with the clay body and its relationship to glaze as she was with form or firing methods. Having worked with wood-firing in Japan, responding to the way the flame and ash interacted with the clay, she regretted that the shortage of this fuel in Cornwall made such firings difficult. Nevertheless, this did not deter her from building a series of small, experimental kilns at St Ives for herself and the other potters. These kilns were used for firing saltglaze stoneware as well as achieving more Bizen-like effects that involved wrapping pots in seaweed, rope and other combustible materials to leave their imprint on the surface. The saltglaze firings tended to meet with limited success, resulting in some pots looking starved of glaze, though it was a process that intrigued Janet, leading her on one occasion to successfully collaborate with the established saltglaze potter Ian Gregory. One early full-bodied thrown bowl with cut sides, made and fired at St Ives, bears the textured surface markings of a saltglaze firing, bringing out the strength of the form.

Like any artist, Janet Leach's pots reflect something of her own life and character, though in a deeply encoded form. Any gendering of her pots would tend towards the masculine, their assured, upright form and stable bases highlighted by their slightly off-centre asymmetry. The use of poured or splashed glaze combined accident with design, recalling the gestural[3] work of artists such as Jackson Pollock, and introduced a further freer note to the shape, a contrast to the usual precision of thrown forms. Such pieces have an assured and relaxed confidence, suggesting a maker at ease with herself, confident in handling clay and glaze. Over the years, while willingly carrying out such 'masculine' tasks as preparing clay, chopping wood and firing kilns, paradoxically, she integrated her studio and her home in a more 'feminine' manner.[4] From the start of her career as an artist Janet had forged her own independent identity, whether as a sculptor or as one of the few women to train as a potter in Japan, suggesting that she was someone with a strong sense of her own identity.

The shape of the triangular pottery stamp used to impress her name on the pots made at St Ives was intrigu-

ABOVE: Janet Leach – Bottle, coiled and thrown, stoneware, 1979, H about 21cm

ingly autobiographical. While bearing the simplified initials JL, the triangle – distinctive, distinguished and curiously western – was carefully chosen. The potter's stamp, adopted from the idea of the 'chop' or seal of China, is usually square in form and used as a signature on a work of art. Janet's securely-balanced geometrical form owed more to ancient Greece or Egypt than the Far East. The three-sided form can also be seen to signify the three parts of Janet Leach's life – one in America, one in Japan, the other in Britain – or her sexual identity, which included passionate attachments to both men and women.

Yet the chief reason for Janet to choose the triangular form was to convey some of the ideas and teaching that she

Introduction | 9

ABOVE TOP: Rudolf Steiner

ABOVE BOTTOM: Jar, Tamba, natural glaze, Muromachi period, H43cm

[5] 1895-1978
[6] Quoted in W A Ismay, 'Pottery by Janet Leach', Southover Gallery, Lewes, February 1981, Crafts, no. 50, May/June 1981
[7] Quoted in Gerry Williams, 'Janet Leach: American Foreigner', The Studio Potter, vol. 11, no. 2, June 1983, pp76-92
[8] Quoted in J P Hodin, 'Janet Darnell Leach', Pottery Quarterly, vol. 9, no. 33, Autumn 1967, p11
[9] For a useful description of the qualities of Japanese pottery see Soame Jenyns, Japanese Pottery, Faber and Faber, London, 1971
[10] Janet Leach, 'Shoji Hamada', Ceramic Review, no. 101, September/October 1986, pp26-27

had became familiar with at Threefold Farm, a Steiner community where she established her first pottery workshop. Rudolf Steiner was the founder of Goetheanum, the centre of anthroposophy, a philosophical movement that stressed the spiritual rather than the materialistic and mechanistic aspects of life. Steiner identified a three-part progression for the human soul, the Sentient or Sensation Soul (*Empfindungsseele*), the Intellectual or Mind Soul (*Verstandseele*), and the Consciousness or Spiritual Soul (*Bewusstseinseele*), a trinity that Janet found a useful way of shaping her life, hence the design of her stamp. While not dissimilar to the Christian concept of the Holy Trinity of Father, Son and Holy Spirit, for Steiner it carried no overt religious meaning but was a way of involving the whole person. The three-part concept was also in line with John Ruskin's argument that the best art involves head, heart and hand, an idea taken up by Bernard Leach as a central and vital part of a search for unity.

Introduced to anthroposophy shortly after deciding to become a potter, she found the Steiner community supportive in helping to give understanding and direction to her life, though she found such understanding did not extend to her pots. After meeting the English potter Bernard Leach and the Japanese potter Shoji Hamada,[5] she decided to move to Japan to explore the long but then fast disappearing traditions of country pottery that were still surviving in remote villages in the 1950s. Finding her way as an artist was a slow process. As she pointed out many times, Texas, the state in which she had initially hoped to become an artist, then had no major art collection showing either sculpture or painting and few role models for a young woman in search of an outlet for creative energy. It was only after moving to New York that she found her artistic vocation.

In terms of assessing her success, only on rare occasions did Janet feel that she had achieved what she wanted, such as when, at one of her exhibitions, she was asked about one of her pots and she replied disarmingly, 'I don't remember making that; I think it grew'.[6] It was a remark that was modest and beguiling, resisting any intellectualisation of her work. When discussing her pots and the ideas that informed them she was equally modest, claiming that she had 'no secondary motives... I have seen and heard and studied many philosophies. Even the beautiful concept of "the Unknown Craftsman" – the primitive pots that none of us can make – doesn't lead me to espouse a special philosophy to pass on to other potters.' With pragmatic understanding, she said 'I just make my pots... I don't care what kind of kiln you have, or how you fire it, the variations of the sphere are unlimited. The good pot is not one kind of pot, but many. I am quite satisfied with the pursuit of that good pot'.[7]

Of modern pots, some of the finest for her were made by Hamada. His quiet, unassuming approach, Zen-based philosophy and the calmness and understatement of his work remained a lasting influence on her ideas. 'Hamada's pots sit there like a beautiful stone, self sufficient', she said. 'You can pass it by like a natural object, without any device for technical perfection'.[8]

From working in country potteries in Japan she had first-hand experience of Japanese concepts such as *wabi*, *sabi* and *shibui*, which informed the pots she admired. Such qualities could be freely translated as austerity and sobriety, often expressed in pottery as the freedom from precise forms, a richness in simple irregularities and escape from restraint (*kishiku*), suggesting an absence of awareness rather than consciously sought qualities. Unglazed vessels scarred by fire or wood ash are often seen to possess such qualities.[9] Although resistant to philosophising about her pots or her Zen Buddhist aesthetic, she did note a *shibui* moment when visiting an exhibition of Hamada's pots in 1954. 'There sat about seventy-five pots that I knew individually quite well, but a room full was something else. They just sat there like stones by the river-bed. They did not perform, they did not reach out and grab you, they were fulfilled within themselves and did not seem to care whether you liked them or not. These were his "shibui" pots'.[10]

In addition to the work of Hamada and the potters she worked with in Japan, Janet also came to admire the hand-built pots made by First Nation American potters in the area now known as Mexico and the equally powerful sixteenth and seventeenth century rustic looking, full-bodied wares from sites in Japan such as Bizen, Karatsu and Iga.

ABOVE TOP: Flower vase, Iga, Momoyama period, H28cm

ABOVE BOTTOM: Shoji Hamada – Bottle, press-moulded, stoneware, c1980, H about 16cm

ABOVE TOP: Flower vase, Bizen, Momoyama period, H26cm

ABOVE BOTTOM: Janet Leach – Jar with lug handles, coiled and thrown, red stoneware, c1990, H about 9cm (Photo: Jason Wason; Collection: Joanna Wason)

OPPOSITE PAGE: Janet Leach – Jar with lug handles, coiled and thrown, red stoneware, c1990, H about 9cm (Photo: Jason Wason; Collection: Joanna Wason)

Such Japanese pots were often irregular in form with little glaze, the body often bearing the marks of the flame and smoke from the firing. Bizen, in South Honshu on the shores of the Inland Sea of Japan, was renowned for its wares made in the local reddish-brown clay that often had surfaces resembling the effects of saltglaze. This was reputed to have been achieved by throwing seaweed on the fire, a technique that was to inspire experiments at St Ives with a small kiln. The irregular but controlled forms made at Karatsu, introduced initially by Korean immigrant potters, were intended for daily use. As an indication of their unassuming qualities the bowls were adopted by tea masters for their quiet beauty and textured and often crawled glazes. Iga was well-known for freely thrown shapes and rough textured surface, the water pots, which often had splits or cracks, being highly prized by tea masters. One tall form, with a smaller collar, rounded neck and tiny lug handles resembling a figure, was a great inspiration for Janet.[11]

Writing about Janet's pots, Bernard Leach believed that 'the pot is the man (or woman)', linking them to the character of the maker. Janet's 'natural character' he saw as 'strong and independent', qualities clearly evident in her pots. 'She was a sculptor before she took up pottery and worked on a large scale so one finds in her pottery breadth, size and good organisation of clay, glaze and fire… her best work is quite distinctive and makes a definite contribution to the pottery of our period'.[12] It is that contribution which is the subject of this book.

---

[11] See plate 32a, for instance, in Soame Jenyns, *Japanese Pottery*, Faber and Faber, London, 1971
[12] Quoted in J P Hodin, 'Janet Darnell Leach', *Pottery Quarterly*, vol. 9, no. 33, Autumn 1967, p13

1 Lone Star State
Texas 1918-37

ABOVE TOP: Morton Salt Co., Grand Saline

ABOVE BOTTOM: Ginning Day, Grand Saline, c1905

OPPOSITE PAGE: Janet Leach – Bottle, coiled and thrown, poured glaze, red stoneware, c1980, H46cm (Photo: David Westwood; Collection: Crafts Study Centre)

Nell Janet Darnell, the only child of Charles Walter and Ollie Rebecca Darnell, was born on March 15, 1918 in Grand Saline, Texas, shortly before her father entered the US navy. The name Nell seems to have been rapidly forgotten, never appearing on surviving official documents. As she was to proudly point out, her ancestors were pioneering Americans who arrived in Texas from Missouri in covered wagons, stopping fifteen miles from what was later found to be the world's largest oilfield in very deep sand. As a way of expressing her pride in the Lone Star State she often sported a Stetson. Because of its extensive salt mines Grand Saline was known as the 'salt capital of Texas'. In the early decades of the twentieth century it was a settlement of fewer than 3,000 inhabitants, boasting two banks, two weekly newspapers, a lumberyard, an ice plant, two gins, one school and five churches. Fires in 1917 and 1919 damaged local businesses, adding to the general economic depression. Within such a small conservative community there was no opportunity for a liberal, let alone a more specialist, art education.

It was a modest family home. Her father, a trained accountant with Mobil oil, had left his job because of problems with his eyes and subsequently took a number of less well-paid positions. These included driving a lorry and working as a clerk in a drug store, where he was liked, not least because he could keep efficient records. For a time the family moved to the state capital, Dallas, remaining there until Janet was in the second year of high school, when they returned to Grand Saline. It was not a particularly happy childhood. Her parents, devout Methodists, were strict and, to Janet, narrow-minded and prejudiced. As an only child she was often left to amuse herself; a

ABOVE TOP: Janet Leach – Jar, hand-built, stoneware, 1979, H about 12cm

ABOVE BOTTOM: Janet Leach – Bottle with lug handles, coiled and thrown, black stoneware, c1980, H about 30cm (Photo: Peter Kinnear)

[1] The Exposition ran from June 6 to November 29, 1936

favourite pastime was whittling wood and other materials that came to hand. For this she was able to make use of the plentiful supply of sharp knives dropped by some of those arrested by her grandfather, who was a sergeant in the police department, which were collected from the floor of the police wagon. After leaving school, in search of independence and keen to pursue a career as an artist, or more precisely a sculptor, she returned to Dallas to stay with her Aunt Billie Jones, of whom she was fond.

In the state capital, for a time Janet attended a small local art school that had recently been started in a fine old house where the lessons included life drawing classes. Charcoal sketches were made of men wearing discreet posing pouches and nude female models. When the female models failed to turn up local prostitutes were called upon to pose, only too pleased to be paid 'just for doing nothing'. Her mother, however, hearing of the classes, disapproved of her daughter attending the school and Janet was only rescued from returning to the family home by obtaining a job as a sculptural assistant making dioramas that set out the history of the state. These were for the 1936 Texas Centennial Exposition, a world fair held at Fair Park in Dallas, to celebrate the 100th anniversary of Texan independence from Mexico.[1] The event attracted over six million visitors; the Cavalcade of Texas, a historical pageant covering four centuries of Texan history, proving to be one of the most popular attractions.

With a friend named Sarah, Janet helped Spanish refugees fleeing from the war in Spain on their journey to Mexico. As no ships sailed direct to Mexico the refugees landed in New York and travelled south through Texas. Sarah's house was used as a stopping-off point where refugees could eat and rest before moving on to special centres in San Antonio. Janet's artistic flair was called upon to make posters and help organise the efforts, while conversations with the refugees helped her learn Spanish and introduced her first-hand to the radical politics that had caused such upheaval in their lives. Whether it was this influence of the war in Spain or the general depressed economy, as part of shaping her life Janet became a communist. Strong-minded and determined to

ABOVE: Janet Leach – Lidded pot, thrown and turned, c1980, H11.5cm (Photo: Phil Rogers; Collection: Phil Rogers)

pursue a career as an artist, at the age of nineteen she decided that to fulfil her desire she needed to move north, taking a range of jobs to earn the necessary funds including one whittling the heads, hands and feet of puppets. Together with a friend, who was married to a geology prospector for Mobil oil, she scraped together the fare of fifty dollars to travel by Greyhound bus to New York, knowing that if the worst came to the worst her friend would be able to pay her rent.

2 A Sculptor in New York
America 1937-49

ABOVE: Janet Leach – Bottle with lug handles, coiled and thrown, stoneware, 1980, H about 40cm (Photo: Peter Kinnear)

OPPOSITE PAGE: Janet Leach – Vase, stoneware, coiled and thrown, poured glaze decoration, reduction fired, c1985, H24cm

[1] Robert M Cronbach (1908-2001) had his first solo show at the Hudson Walker Gallery in New York in 1940, going on to exhibit for many years with the Bertha Shaefer Gallery, New York
[2] Through the Federal Arts Project, the patronage of the arts from 1933 to 1945 resulted in some 3,350 public murals, 18,000 sculptures, 108,000 easel paintings, 250,000 prints, 2 million posters and 500,000 photographs produced in hundreds of federally funded community arts centres and studios

For a young woman barely nineteen, New York must have seemed both full of opportunity and a daunting challenge. With a heavy Texan accent Janet felt 'as much a foreigner in New York' as she was later to experience in Japan or in St Ives. The Depression, the collapse of the stock market and the downfall of the art market did not help secure employment. Even museums and art galleries were forced to run limited exhibition schedules. Janet enrolled in a small art school, where her sculpture teacher was Robert M Cronbach,[1] an artist with a growing reputation for his sensitive handling of the figure in a quietly expressive manner. Cronbach, working on Federal Arts Projects (FAP), carried out large assignments; his commissions included sculptures and fountains at the United Nations General Assembly Building, the Fashion Institute of Technology and the Federal Office Building in St Louis. The FAP, created in 1935 by President Franklin Roosevelt, was part of the New Deal aimed at generating economic reform and job relief while restoring a sense of self to those suffering through the Depression.[2] Arts projects were guided by the assumption that artists were workers and that art was cultural labour worthy of government support. The FAP was seen as a success, creating over 5,000 jobs for artists and resulting in the production of numerous works of art. Despite the Depression it was a period when women artists were able to gain greater public presence; a 1935 survey indicated that forty-one percent of the artists were female.

While New Deal arts patronage was partly to engender unity and restore national confidence in the American economy, it also offered artists solid and real support. The New Deal appealed to the left-leaning young artist and Janet became involved in making large sculptures in

ABOVE: Janet Leach – Bottle, coiled, thrown and beaten, incised decoration, stoneware, c1980, H about 40cm (Photo: Peter Kinnear)

OPPOSITE PAGE: Janet Leach – Bottle, coiled and thrown, red stoneware, 1986, H25cm (Photo: Peter Hoare; Collection: Buckinghamshire County Museum, Aylesbury)

plaster, becoming an efficient mechanic and 'girl Friday', the experience entitling her to FAP funding. 'This was good training for me as I was in the company of all kinds of craftsmen, stonecutters, an old Italian caster and young artists. I thought of myself at that time as an architectural sculptor'.[3]

The outbreak of war in Europe, however distant, was vividly brought home to Janet when, to her disgust, Hitler and Stalin made a non-aggression pact.[4] Given her violent opposition to fascism and her support for Soviet Russia she was appalled and disillusioned by the alliance. The bombing of Pearl Harbor by Japan in December 1941 brought the US into the war and a new sense of reality to the country, ending, for Janet, her work as an artist. By this time she had married an Italian shipyard worker, a skilled technician called Joe Turino, but soon discovered that they had little in common. 'I wasn't being very intelligent', she recalled. To avoid being drafted into the military Turino wanted them to have a child, arguing that being a father would help him escape enlistment, but not particularly wanting to start a family and knowing that such a move would be only a temporary delay, she refused. Equally, however much she supported the war against fascism, her political beliefs made her reluctant to add to the glorification of GIs. With his experience in the shipyard, Turino was soon drafted into the navy with the advantage of a couple of stripes, which effectively brought their marriage to an end.

Keen to join in the war effort, being familiar with the docks and preferring to choose the work she did, Janet took a job in the shipyard working as a civilian with the army in what she described as 'the port of embarkation'. Any romantic idea that war work carried an element of glamour was soon dispelled. The pay was poor and she was under the direction of what she called 'one-day wonders', recently commissioned but inexperienced officers – a situation not to her liking. Tough and physical, the work involved unloading lorries and operating tractors. The crew, of which she was a part, was not allowed to load ships, a job restricted to members of the union, but it was their responsibility to fill lorries that were driven by black drivers. Apart from the exhausting manual labour and the poor administration, the

[3] Quoted in Gerry Williams, 'Janet Leach: American Foreigner', *The Studio Potter*, vol. 11. no. 2, June 1983, pp76-92
[4] A non-aggression pact between Russia and Germany was signed on August 23, 1939. This was broken when Germany invaded Russia

ABOVE: Janet Leach – Bottle, coiled and thrown, poured glaze decoration, red stoneware, 1979, H about 40cm

OPPOSITE PAGE: Janet Leach – Bottle, coiled and thrown stoneware, finger-wipe decoration, 1982, H27cm (Photo: Peter Hoare; Collection: Buckinghamshire County Museum, Aylesbury)

[5] At the beginning of the Second World War it took 196 days to build a Liberty ship; this was reduced to 27 days and by 1943 America turned out one Liberty ship every 18.3 hours. Quoted in Peter Dormer, *The New Ceramics: Trends + Traditions*, Thames and Hudson, 1986, p19

biggest eye-opener was the social issues raised by working alongside black Americans. She was, for instance, horrified to discover that for many of the black workers it was for the first time in their lives that they were being provided with suitable clothing, given free dental treatment, decent housing and supplied with a properly balanced diet.

With war work opening up areas of employment previously thought to be the prerogative of men, Janet saw an opportunity not only to get a better and more challenging job but also to learn a skill that might be useful to her as a sculptor. Bethlehem Steel, on Staten Island, given substantial navy contracts, needed trainee welders and she duly applied for and was recruited alongside nine other women and two black men, every one of whom was a college graduate. The yard built vessels up to 416 feet in length and did repairs on even larger ships. During the war a total of forty-seven destroyers, seventy-five landing craft, five cargo vessels and three ocean-going tugs were built. It was, she recalled, heavy but skilled and rewarding work. The women were given fifteen minutes off every afternoon, though she preferred to work on, happy to compete with the men. With flying colours she duly qualified as a Navy Certified Welder, remaining until the end of the war as a skilled welder working on building some ten hulls, forward assemblies and bows.[5]

Living in the centre of the city and travelling one and a half hours on a crowded journey to Staten Island proved tedious, so when she discovered a houseboat near work that was moored in a quiet and peaceful backwater she, together with two other women, rented it. At much the same time she purchased an army surplus 32cc motorbike that had been standing on the docks waiting to be shipped to troops in the desert. Originally painted a military khaki, she transformed her bike with white refrigerator paint, the only colour available, spraying it piece by piece in the bathroom of the houseboat. Named *Dude*, the motorbike offered freedom and independence. 'We worked hard, there was not much to buy and we needed recreation'.

After the purposeful activity of the war, the peace left Janet feeling as displaced and disorientated as a discharged GI but without any official support to help her readjust.

ABOVE: Janet Leach – Bottle with lug handles, coiled and thrown, stoneware, c1980, H about 45cm (Photo: Peter Kinnear)

[6] Letter to author 1989. n.d.
[7] See Thomas Turnquist, 'New York City Ceramics, Part I, The Inwood Pottery Studios', *American Art Pottery Association Journal*, vol. 1, no. 2, March/April 1985
[8] Lorrie H Goulet, born Riverdale, New York, 1925. Worked with Aimee Voorhees at Inwood Pottery Studios in New York City from 1932 to 1936, later with Josef Albers at the avant-garde Black Mountain College in North Carolina 1943 and 1944
[9] 1899-1973. See Jeff Schlanger and Toshiko Takaezu, *Maija Grotell: Works Which Grow From Belief*, Studio Potter Books, New Hampshire, 1996
[10] Quoted in Gerry Williams, 'Janet Leach: American Foreigner', *The Studio Potter*, vol. 11, no. 2, June 1983, pp76-92
[11] Published 1940 by Faber and Faber.
[12] At this time Janet's address was 896 Third Ave, Apt 7, New York. 22, New York
[13] Janet Darnell letter to Bernard Leach, November 12, 1955. P.C.

Her two houseboat companions, along with many of her art friends, 'got magenta on their palettes' and moved to California. Still intent on a career as a sculptor, she again worked as studio assistant with Cronbach, while at the same time making her own sculpture. These pieces were shown and admired in group exhibitions in a 57th Street gallery but found no buyers and were duly carried back to her fifth floor tenement. Even the satisfaction of having a piece exhibited at the 122nd exhibition of the National Academy of Design in New York failed to lift her spirits. Entitled *Hornblower*, this was laboriously carved from a three-inch diameter of brass 'just to prove it would have been different if modelled and cast'.[6] To supplement her income she took a job as an after-school play worker for the Play School Association helping latch-key children. This involved playing baseball and taking them on trips.

The realisation that succeeding as a sculptor in the post-war climate was difficult for a man, let alone a woman, forced a career rethink. By chance Janet heard about the Inwood Pottery Studios, which had a reputation for thoughtful work, and decided to try clay. The Inwood Studios had originally been set up in the early 1920s by Harry Voorhees and Aimee LePrince Voorhees on the site of an old Indian village called Shorakop-kik in what was then northern Manhattan. When this property was purchased by New York City as part of creating a park the studio moved near to 168th Street, which was where Janet went for two or three years. In addition to making pieces such as plates, lamp bases, tiles, jars and bowls, the Inwood Studios provided a range of ceramic services that included classes for potters, the use of the studio facilities by potters and ceramic sculptors, glazing and firing pots, the making of casts from originals and arranging such things as exhibitions and demonstrations.[7] Aimee Voorhees, as Janet often proudly pointed out, had been awarded a Gold Medal in Paris. Over the years the pottery helped train many artists including the sculptor Lorrie Goulet;[8] the renowned Finnish-born potter Maija Grotell[9] taught there in the thirties. Following Harry Voorhees's death in 1936 the pottery was run by Aimee Voorhees with her sister.

At Inwood Janet learnt basic skills, including throwing, glazing and firing. 'I began making pots as a sort of occupational therapy... I had worked a great deal in clay, painting and enlarging architectural pieces. Pottery seemed a step down. Nevertheless, I got a tremendous satisfaction when I made a bowl and someone put potatoes in it, although I wasn't naturally a utilitarian potter'.[10] Intending to enjoy pottery as a hobby rather than as a profession, she was soon enamoured by the qualities of clay, its ability to be shaped and formed in the kiln and by the fact that making was defined by a specific function and purpose. The two sisters, by then old and arthritic, taught rather than made pots but they did lend Janet their copy of the first edition of Bernard Leach's *A Potter's Book*.[11] This volume was distinguished from later editions by having the colour plates pasted onto the pages. Faithfully promising to return the precious volume Janet read and was enraptured by the ideas Leach put forward, responding to his arguments for wholeness and unity and by the idea that being a potter was a way of life.[12]

With her new found potting skills Janet took the post of pottery instructor in the occupational therapy department at Rockland State Mental Hospital, New York State's biggest mental institution, twenty miles outside the city. Her contract stated that she 'would plan to teach fundamentals in pottery' as well as help set up the pottery studio. It was a time to consolidate her skills and, like any new teacher, it involved a steep learning curve in discovering, among other things, how much she still had to find out. She remained at Rockland for three years, by which time any involvement in left-wing causes had all but disappeared. Realising that she wanted to pursue a career as a potter but not in an amateur way, she decided to leave her fifth floor tenement flat and move to the country, renting a cabin in the Steiner community at Threefold Farm, Spring Valley, which she had stumbled on by accident. Adopting, as she later wrote to Leach 'the Christian impulse in which love was brought into the world',[13] her life was set to take a different direction.

ABOVE TOP: Bernard Leach – *A Potter's Book*

ABOVE BOTTOM: Janet Leach – Lidded pot, thrown, faceted sides, red stoneware, 1979, H about 12cm

A Sculptor in New York

3 The Human Being as the Universe
Threefold Farm 1949-54

ABOVE: Threefold Farm

Threefold Farm, based on the ideas and teaching of Rudolf Steiner,[1] was the first anthroposophical community in America. It was established in 1922 on 300 acres of land in Spring Valley some thirty miles from New York City. Steiner's inscription, written specifically for the founding of Threefold, can roughly be translated from the German as:

> *Look into the outside world, and find yourself;*
> *look into the depths within yourself, and find the outside world.*
> *If you mark the pendulum swing between yourself and the universe,*
> *then you will discover:*
> *the human being as the universe;*
> *the universe as the human being.*

The farm, then under the leadership of Ralph Courtney, was an experiment in the three-fold social order of community living. The shared system of beliefs included the pursuit of biodynamic farming, a method of agriculture that sought to actively work with the health-giving forces of nature by non-chemical means, and the development of the Steiner education system. This, based on a holistic approach, balanced artistic, academic and practical work to educate the whole child, hand and heart as well as mind. Its innovative methodology and developmentally oriented curriculum permeated with the arts, addressed the changing consciousness of the child, cultivating imagination and creativity as well as cognitive growth alongside a sense of responsibility for the earth and its inhabitants. Although never fully embracing the anthroposophist philosophy, Janet was attracted by the threefold concept and the community spirit, finding the farm a

---

[1] Rudolf Steiner (1861-1925) was the Austrian founder of anthroposophy. He evolved a study of spiritual concerns opposed to conventional occultism; his educational theories of using the arts therapeutically were widely influential
[2] Quoted in Gerry Williams, 'Janet Leach: American Foreigner', *The Studio Potter*, vol. 11, no. 2, June 1983, pp76-92
[3] Charles M Harder (1899-1959), head of ceramics at Alfred University, 1938-58
[4] Quoted in Gerry Williams, 'Janet Leach: American Foreigner', *The Studio Potter*, vol. 11, no. 2, June 1983, pp76-92
[5] March 1950

welcome refuge from the impersonal existence in New York. Here she felt she could develop as a rounded person.

At Threefold Farm Janet was known as Jan, a warm and friendly diminutive she liked; later, in Japan, she bemoaned the return to what she saw as the more formal Janet. At the farm she built her own house and pottery by a brook. 'I cleared the land, did a lot of digging and what building I couldn't do alone I assisted with'.[2] Here she lived with her dog Pecos and her partner Mary Dailey, an educationalist who was busy establishing Green Meadow School. This was based on Steiner principles of education, and Dailey was anxious to build up the number of pupils. Evidently she was successful for the school continues to this day. Threefold Farm proved an ideal setting in which to live and make pots. Janet rebuilt an old downdraught gas kiln, about 10 cubic foot in size, in which she fired earthenware to around 1060°C, finding that it would not go higher because 'the chimney will not stand more heat'. A plan to add an outside wood-burning stoneware kiln was never fulfilled because of her move to Japan. In exchange for the use of the land she gave pottery classes in the afternoon.

One summer, on leave from the hospital, she attended a course at Alfred University, the first occasion she had spent time with serious studio potters. The class, given by Marion Fosdick, included John Kenny – who, she recalled, carefully noted down all Charles M Harder's[3] lectures – Minnie Nagoro, Susan Peterson and Lyle and Dorothy Perkins. 'It was an active, vital time – six weeks with hardly any sleep'.[4] At Alfred, Janet began to see 'the depth of my involvement in pottery, and not just as a future occupation'. When Bernard Leach toured America in 1950, spending several weeks teaching at Alfred University, she attended his public lecture in New York,[5] given when he was presented with the Binn's Medal. Being familiar with his ideas from reading *A Potter's Book*, Janet found the lecture relevant and enthralling.

The years at Threefold Farm were fulfilling both mentally and creatively; the community provided a structure within which she could explore a social and moral consciousness while discovering a direction for her own life. As a rebellious though not anarchic artist, Janet found a new and

ABOVE TOP: Charles Harder working on wheel, Alfred University

ABOVE BOTTOM: Janet Leach – Lidded pot, coiled and thrown, incised decoration, stoneware, c1980, H about 15cm

ABOVE TOP: Black Mountain College, seminar advertisement, 1952

ABOVE BOTTOM: Black Mountain College advertisement

OPPOSITE: Janet Leach – Bottle, coiled and thrown, faceted sides, stoneware, 1979, H about 21cm

[6] To Ralph Courtney, August 26, 1954. P.C.
[7] Letter to Miss Canfield, a friend in the USA, November 26, 1954
[8] Janet Leach, 'Shoji Hamada', *Ceramic Review*, no. 101, September/October 1986, pp26-27
[9] *Mingei* is the term for folk art, objects made by anonymous craftsmen to be used as part of rural life, their beauty coming from making
[10] Potter and educator, studied at the Bauhaus, Germany, moved to America just before the Second World War

meaningful vitality. Some sense of the support she felt at Threefold is conveyed in a letter she later wrote to a friend who was living there: 'I personally am greatly appreciative of the farm and its process of throwing the individual upon himself, forcing some degree of self-knowledge for survival.'[6] In another letter she spoke of finding the Farm 'delightful', adding 'but it must be lived in to be appreciated – it doesn't show its basic character in casual visits. I have found great warmth and friendship there; at the same time, there is complete freedom for the individual and one's privacy is never imposed on – an amazing balance between the two – the fact that many have lived together for 20 years in harmony speaks for itself.'[7]

Yet, despite the security, support and acceptance within the community she felt something was not right with her pots, though what she could not identify. Leach's ideas had opened new worlds, offering alternative ways of approaching pots, but she did not fully understand how to do this, writing: 'I... spent two years by a brook, with the help of Bernard Leach's *A Potter's Book*, trying to find the mystery of the "good pot". I was feeling defeated and dissatisfied with my work'.[8]

Two years after first hearing Leach lecture she found he was again visiting the States, on this occasion with the Japanese potter Shoji Hamada and the *Mingei*[9] philosopher/critic Soetsu Yanagi to teach a two-week course at Black Mountain College, from October 15-29, 1952. The seminar was to be hosted by Marguerite Wildenhain,[10] a potter who had trained at the Bauhaus, designed for the ceramics industry and ran a pottery in California. Janet, along with one or two friends, was keen to attend, even though this meant scrimping together funds both for the 700 mile journey to Ashville, North Carolina and the course fees.

Black Mountain had a justified reputation as a progressive college pushing at the boundaries of different arts disciplines. It was renowned for its experimental, interdisciplinary approach, and was a major invigorating force within American culture. Unlike other colleges it was led by practising artists and craftsmen and women and became the centre for many of the new, radical ideas in dance and the visual arts. It was also beautifully situated, and, at 2500

ABOVE TOP: Black Mountain College, (L-R) Shoji Hamada, Bernard Leach, Soetsu Yanagi, Marguerite Wildenhain, 1952 (Leach Archive, Crafts Study Centre)

ABOVE BOTTOM: Shoji Hamada working on the wheel, c1970

OPPOSITE: Janet Leach – Bottle, coiled and thrown, black body, poured glaze, 1980, H16cm

[11] For a full account see Edmund de Waal 'The event of a thread, the event of clay: Black Mountain College and the Crafts', in *Starting at Zero: Black Mountain College 1933-57*, Caroline Collier and Michael Harrison, Arnolfini, Bristol/ Kettle's Yard, Cambridge, 2005
[12] Quoted in Gerry Williams, 'Janet Leach: American Foreigner', *The Studio Potter*, vol. 11, no. 2, June 1983, pp76-92
[13] Ibid.
[14] Ibid.
[15] Susan Peterson, 'Bernard Leach: Two Recollections', *The Studio Potter*, vol. 8, no. 1, 1979-80, p3
[16] Bernard Leach, 'The American Journey with Yanagi and Hamada'. n.d. P.C.

feet, the setting was magnificent. At this time of year the mountains were covered in brilliant autumn colours.

Under the heading 'eastern center for interchange of work and ideas east to west', the seminar promised a great deal, with topics ranging from 'the development of form ideas', design for mass production and craft in the machine world, to the thorny topic of the relationship of craft to art, highlighting some of the main concerns for crafts in the middle of the twentieth century. Such dualities as the Bauhaus and Japan, the pragmatic and philosophical, were brought uneasily together.[11]

For Janet the big attraction was seeing and hearing Leach, and she later confessed that she knew nothing about Japanese pots and felt no direct connection with their aesthetic. The war had resulted in an understandable prejudice in the generation involved in the Spanish Civil war, the Japanese conquest of China and the bombing of Pearl Harbor, with Janet feeling that 'the East Coast had been fighting Hitler and the West Coast fighting the Japanese'. To consider travelling a vast distance to hear two Japanese experts involved quite a different mindset.

Films, slide shows, demonstrations, lectures, parties, excursions and social events were planned for the thirty-five enthusiastic students and potters who attended. The three star lecturers soon assumed their roles. Leach 'tall and gangly in his homespun tweeds, woollen socks, heavy brogues and separate collars'[12] took charge, the 'articulator, the innovator… who coupled standards with form'. He talked a great deal, smoked, waved his arms about and, occasionally, made pots. By contrast Hamada 'short, round and jolly-looking, in Japanese work clothes and vegetable-dyed homespun',[13] said little, spoke only Japanese even though he was fluent in English and focused on making, working on and off the wheel. In rapt silence the students watched as he sat cross-legged and threw on the wheel, later assembling a teapot from parts he had made in a matter of minutes.

After the practical approach of the two potters, Yanagi, 'petite and very much the international gentleman with his silver-headed cane'[14] and 'master of Zen aesthetics',[15] spoke on Buddhist theories of beauty and Zen and Shin – 'the road of the few and the road of the many'[16] – challenging

ABOVE: Hamada throwing a pot, Mashiko, 1954

abstract concepts that often went above the heads of their audience. With titles such as 'The Responsibilities of Criticism', the three sought to convey their approach to making, appreciating and understanding pots and the role of tradition within contemporary society. Clamours for copies of Yanagi's talk suggest that many students required time and thought to digest its ideas and concepts.

The seminar was an introduction into a new world, one in which the 'good pot' took on moral as well as aesthetic qualities. However, the biggest surprise for Janet was seeing Hamada at work on the wheel, later describing it as 'the most important experience of my life'.[17] Spellbound, she watched as he sat cross-legged at the potter's wheel, untroubled by the audience, seemingly oblivious of the hungry eyes watching his every move as he dipped only his fingers in the muddy water and patted and pulled the clay as if coaxing out its sensual, generous qualities. 'He was making the richest and warmest pots I have ever seen. He was like a child, almost as if he were playing patty cake... Hamada's way on the wheel was gentle and easy.[18] His technique for making a large pot was to 'beat a hole in the centre of the mound of clay with one hand as he patted the outside with the other. One or two passes brought it up, wavering, going blub blub and you thought he was going to lose it, but suddenly it is pulled together and comes out even at the top.'[19]

Later, she wrote 'when Hamada is throwing, it is obvious that he is conscious only of the nature of the material that he is using – clay – and the form that he is envisioning... He is striving for the spirit of the form in clay, the pots come up and at the first spontaneous burst of life he stops working it... he does not sacrifice spontaneous vitality for the sake of mechanical slickness and perfection.'[20] By comparison Leach, sitting upright at the wheel, seemed stiff and formal, and his pots tight and controlled.

The discussions at Black Mountain were dominated by the seemingly disparate themes of tradition and modernity, with all three speakers talking about the broad base of their aesthetic ideas, their concern with unity of past and present and their all-encompassing philosophical approach. While some students found their preference for soft, muted earth colours and harmonious shapes dull and old-

[17] Letter to author, 1989. n.d.
[18] Quoted in Gerry Williams, 'Janet Leach: American Foreigner', *The Studio Potter*, vol. 11, no. 2, June 1983, pp76-92
[19] Janet Leach, 'Shoji Hamada', *Ceramic Review*, no. 101, September/October 1986, pp26-27
[20] Janet Leach, 'With Hamada in Mashiko' *Pottery Quarterly*, vol. 3, no. 11, Autumn 1956, pp97-102

ABOVE: Janet Leach – Bottle, coiled and thrown, incised decoration, stoneware, 1979, H about 20cm

fashioned, to Janet they made complete sense. She was also intrigued by Hamada's insistence on the pleasure of self-sufficiency and 'rootedness', expressed through the use of local materials, as he explained how attractive stoneware glazes could be made from combinations of rock and wood ash and demonstrated how bundles of grass could be bound to make useful brushes.

Strong-willed, resolute and undeterred by the eminence of the guests, Janet argued fiercely with them, particularly with Leach over what she saw as his lack of comprehension of the country's cultural make-up. Few Americans, she pointed out, even began to comprehend his concept of tradition and far from revering the past as a virtue many equated it with old-fashioned fuddy-duddy habits unrelated to modern needs. There was also the question of First

ABOVE TOP: Janet Leach – Teabowls, thrown, poured glaze decoration, stoneware, c1980, H about 7cm

ABOVE BOTTOM: (L-R) Richard Hieb, Janet Darnell, Shoji Hamada, 1954

Nation pottery, which, with its strong hand-built forms and integrated surface decoration, was recognised as making an important contribution to the concept of tradition within modern America. But, as Janet was quick to point out, she was not Indian and while admiring the qualities of the ware did not, at that time, see it as part of her inheritance. Fiercely, she also rejected work made by immigrant studio potters from England, which to her seemed 'awful'.

Through such vigorous debate, interspersed with dancing and socialising, a friendship began, with Leach, who responded to Janet's enthusiasm, finding 'her mind alive and intelligent'.[21] Vivacious and confident, with striking angular features and a mop of dark, curly hair, Susan Peterson remembers her as 'wiry, bony, thin with deep-set eyes... fun-loving and happy'.[22]

While Leach's ideas and charismatic manner made a big impression, it was Hamada who seemed more important and relevant, his approach to making pots persuading her that she must experience this living tradition at first-hand. 'I was more or less self-taught... and still did not feel I understood what pottery was about'. Her pots, she felt, were 'too mechanical' and that she used the wheel too much like a lathe without fully realising its potential as an expressive medium. The idea of working with Hamada in Japan was a challenge, not only because of her own limited financial resources but because, conventionally, women there did not train as potters. Richard Hieb,[23] a fellow student at Black Mountain asked, without hesitation, if he could work with Hamada at Mashiko and was accepted. Fearing a refusal, Janet was reluctant to speak about her plan, thinking that it might be wise to take time to think about both the practical and philosophical implications.

Back in Spring Valley, after a time to 'cool down', but with the vivid memory of the lively conversation and the sense of completeness that surrounded Hamada, she wrote to Leach in Japan asking about the possibilities of her working with Hamada. Receiving no reply she wrote again, doubting if her request had been taken seriously. She outlined her experience of living in a Steiner community, her involvement with anthroposophy and her search for some sort of meaning and feeling in her pots. Thinking that the

[21] Bernard Leach, *Beyond East and West*, Faber and Faber, London 1978, p245
[22] Interview with author, March 21, 1997
[23] Born 1931

ABOVE: Janet Leach – Bottle, coiled, thrown and beaten, black stoneware, c1980, H about 30cm (Photo: Peter Kinnear)

Japanese judge character by handwriting and doubtful if hers would meet with approval, she elected to type her letters, a skill she had acquired, mindful also that Leach was writing a book about his experiences in Japan and may need secretarial assistance. At last Leach did reply and a regular correspondence ensued.

One difficulty, as Janet had previously observed, was the lowly status of women in comparison to men. While Richard Hieb's application had been successful, it took

ABOVE TOP: Janet Leach – Jar with lug handles, poured glaze decoration, stoneware, 1979, H about 14cm

OPPOSITE: Janet Leach – Bowl on pedestal with lug handles, coiled and thrown, black stoneware, c1980, H35cm (Photo: Peter Kinnear)

much deliberation before Hamada, at Leach's urging, approved her request.[24] Finally Hamada agreed not only to sponsor her but also to offer accommodation in the gatehouse at his pottery. The letter, approving her visit, arrived in January 1954, throwing Janet into a frenzy of activity. 'I had ten dollars in the bank at the time, so I had to scratch around a bit'.[25] With the full support of the Threefold community she sought to raise funds, taking a job designing fluorescent light fixtures and making pots. Among other objects she made a wren's nesting box. 'They were designed in the shape of a hornet's nest, cast whole and suspended by a piece of rope. Squirrels couldn't get at them, Woodpeckers couldn't peck holes and let in the squirrels. You didn't have to take them down or do anything.'[26] The birds quickly adopted the nest, the small opening preventing other birds from entering.[27] They were a great success.

A woman in a local grocery shop cleared a corner for Janet to display her pots and several friends contributed to her fund-raising activities. In ten weeks she earned an impressive $1,000, sufficient for her to manage modestly for two years. On the assumption that she would return the pottery was closed but left intact.[28] A passage was booked on the cargo boat *Canada Mail*, the cheapest fare, and Janet arrived at Yokohama on June 3, 1954 in pouring rain, discovering, to her delight, that the men on the quay were dressed in traditional straw raincoats. Her new life had begun.

[24] February 1954, agreeing she could arrive in the summer
[25] Quoted in Gerry Williams, 'Janet Leach: American Foreigner', *The Studio Potter*, vol. 11, no. 2, June 1983. pp76-92
[26] Interview with author, St Ives, February 10, 1996
[27] There are plans to remake the nesting boxes from moulds of original boxes (2005)
[28] At one point during her time in Japan there were plans to let the pottery, but the scheme never materialised

4 Pottery Heaven
Japan 1954-55

ABOVE: *Mingeikan*, Tokyo

Japan, in seeking to modernise while still having regard for age-old traditions, was a mass of bewildering contradictions, as Janet soon found. Fortunately Leach agreed to meet her at the Takumi craft shop in Tokyo and proved a helpful and thoughtful guide for the next seven days, taking her on a whirlwind tour of the capital's crowded streets, showing her old buildings and escorting her around the *Mingeikan*, the Japanese Folk Craft Museum. This treasure-house, with its magnificent examples of traditional work, from pots to textiles, wood-carving to lacquer work, was a delight. He introduced her to friends such as the Livingstons, through whom she met the French painter Donatienne Lebovitch, who subsequently offered Janet the use of her house whenever she came to Tokyo. Lebovitch, whose husband spent much time in Korea on business, lived in a beautiful traditional Japanese house but, rather than sitting on the floor or sleeping on a futon, preferred Western-style living and so had beds, chairs and a couch. Over the following two years Lebovitch's home was a welcoming bolt-hole where Janet could sleep comfortably in a bed and converse in English.

As Leach had foretold in his letters, Janet soon became aware of the rapid changes that were taking place in Japanese society, particularly in the capital, as the urge to ape the West led to the rejection of many traditional ways, with, as she reported: 'plastic taking the place of porcelain, loud speakers at every corner, in every train and station, radios blasting, horns honking incessantly, raw nude shows – the motto is if it's Western it's good, if it's Japanese it's old fashioned'.[1] Nevertheless, as she discovered, many potters still worked in traditional ways using long-established techniques, whether in making, decorating, glazing or firing pots.

[1] Letter to Miss Parker January 6, 1955. P.C.
[2] For a full description of pottery making at Hamada's pottery see Janet Leach, 'With Hamada in Mashiko', *Pottery Quarterly*, vol. 3, no. 11, Autumn 1956, pp97-102
[3] Quoted in Yoshiko Uchida 'To Learn Local Methods', *Nippon Times*. n.d. (c. July 1954) P.C.

After all the excitement and contradictions of Tokyo it was a relief to travel with Leach to Mashiko,[2] a distance of some twenty miles, though with a driver who drove at reckless speed, blowing his horn and flying a red flag, she felt more like royalty than a student potter. At Mashiko they were met by a bevy of reporters who plied her with questions. A chic young female reporter had great difficulty in understanding why Janet, a young and attractive woman, wanted to work in a small, unassuming Japanese town when she could enjoy the more sophisticated life of Fifth Avenue. The next day's newspaper carried an article headed 'Blue-eyed potter comes to study at Mashiko'. In another interview, Janet was forthright in stating her case, saying: 'America may have gained the world, but I think she has lost her soul. Americans have lost contact with nature and are now instinctively seeking a return to the land. That's why so many of us are going to Japan'.[3]

In contrast to the capital, Mashiko was a haven, 'a small, unpretentious village which has produced the kitchen ware

ABOVE TOP: Janet Darnell working on the wheel, Tamba, 1954

ABOVE BOTTOM: Fired kiln, Mashiko

Pottery Heaven | **39**

ABOVE TOP: Hamada's gatehouse, Mashiko

ABOVE BOTTOM: Mashiko, 1954

OPPOSITE: Hamada with pots outside kiln, Mashiko, c1975

for Tokyo for about 250 years'.[4] The potteries were mostly small, family businesses still making a range of domestic pots for use in the home. Hamada, attracted by the unpretentious quality of the traditional pots, had settled here in the mid 1920s and, as he prospered, had built a modest estate of traditional houses, acquiring them as they fell into disuse, dismantling and re-erecting them with meticulous care. Such buildings included a gatehouse, where Janet had rooms. This, she wrote, was 'built of heavy timbers, unpainted, with white plaster walls inside and out. The roofs are thick thatch at least 2 feet thick extending out 5 to 6 feet over the building. The roof lines are the most magnificent organic forms I have ever seen and the buildings fit and enhance the landscape and become part of it, rather than stuck on… I knew I was to have one wing of the "gate house" but had no conception of what that meant… There is a flower arrangement and a *kakemoa*, mats on the floor, paper-covered windows which give a beautiful warm light, and sliding panels for doors which enable me to open up half the wall space.'[5]

It was not only the accommodation that was a delight but also the relaxed yet industrious atmosphere in the pottery with the team, consisting of Hamada, his two sons and about half a dozen workers, working together. Fascinated, she watched as they swiftly glazed and then packed the pots in the eight-chamber kiln. 'All day I watched Hamada and his temporarily enlarged crew glazing about 2,000 pots for a firing, starting tomorrow. This was a sight to behold! Pots everywhere – on long boards on the ground, inside – outside. Everyone working happily with an ease and naturalness, complete harmony and compatibility. They have a great working respect for Hamada, not catering to him, not worshipping, just anticipating his needs… They worked until quite late in the evening with still the exuberance and buoyancy of the morning, just doing the job to be done, unselfconsciously.'[6] A large celebration dinner after the two-day firing included several kinds of fish, both raw and cooked, beer and warm saki. Although made welcome, Janet was aware that she was highly privileged, as it was probably the first time they had had a woman at their table. 'Never before have I been so conscious of being a woman',[7] she wrote.

[4] Janet Leach, 'With Hamada in Mashiko', *Pottery Quarterly*, vol. 3, no. 11, Autumn 1956, pp97-102
[5] Japanese diary, 1954. P.C.
[6] Ibid.
[7] Ibid.

ABOVE TOP: Mashiko, 1954

ABOVE BOTTOM: Hamada decorating a pot, Mashiko, 1954

OPPOSITE: Shoji Hamada decorating pots, surrounded by his family, c1975

[8] Diary – 'My First Three Weeks in Japan', 1954. P.C.

The time at Mashiko involved observing rather than doing. Occasionally she was given basic tasks such as grinding the bases of pots – which was an opportunity to handle them – and pressing clay into moulds, but, soon in tune with the mood of the pottery, she longed to be making pots. Recalling her days as a sculptor she did make small clay figures, which were described in a contemporary newspaper article as 'sensitive', though none have subsequently come to light. Her introduction to Japanese culture included a five-hour performance of *Bunraku* puppets where 'the puppets took on so such life and vitality that one was hardly aware of the operators' and a visit to a Zen shrine, with its 'element of restraint (*shibui*)'. During a trip with Leach, Yanagi and his wife, Kaneko, to the newly opened Hakone Museum, which was filled with early Japanese painting and pottery, they were treated as celebrities. Afterwards, at a traditional inn, the food was served on a twelve-inch high table. By convention, women were expected to kneel as 'ladies never sit cross-legged', a position Janet found impossible.

Hamada remained a source of wonderment. Whether seeing him at work on the wheel or stopping to deal patiently with a constant stream of visitors only to resume immediately after they left, calm and unruffled, was to see an artist at one with himself. Much of his throwing was done in his home with the family around him, watching and talking to him while he maintained an air of quiet composure. 'He spins his wheel by hand and throws his large beautiful pots with an ease and flow that is unimaginable. As I watch I get the impression that suddenly the clay takes life and form. It seems that when the pot breathes its first breath he stops, he does not over-work or labour it.'[8]

Mashiko, however, proved more difficult than Janet had imagined, for, despite the magic of watching Hamada, enjoying the industrious but relaxed atmosphere and the welcoming hospitality, she sensed he was reluctant to take her as a student and was keeping her at a distance. Rather than encourage her to make pots he continued to suggest that she observe and at times seemed disinclined even to talk to her. Whether he was uneasy about the fact that she was a woman or that he did not want her to be there is not clear. To add to Janet's confusion there was a certain

ABOVE: Bernard Leach, Janet Darnell, Japan, 1954

[9] Published in the West as *A Potter In Japan: 1952-54*, Faber and Faber, London, 1960
[10] Ogata Kenzan (1663-1743) created a new style of decorated pottery
[11] 1890-1966, leading Japanese individual potter
[12] Planned as an account of the beauty and techniques of pottery from all over the world, the book was never completed, for Yanagi had a disabling stroke shortly after Leach's return to England, though he was able to work on other projects
[13] *Mattcha* is powdered green tea used in the traditional Japanese tea ceremony. Because the whole tea leaf is used, mattcha has a bright green colour, bitter taste and high caffeine content

amount of jealousy from Richard Hieb, who, Janet suspected, viewed her as an unwelcome rival.

With a growing sense of frustration with her role at Hamada's pottery, she was greatly relieved when Leach invited her to accompany him as his secretary on a tour of the country, though it did mean travelling rather than potting. This was a unique opportunity to meet other potters and curators, always difficult without introductions, and to visit remote country potteries and see museums. Such a tour would be problematic on her own, not only because she spoke or read no Japanese but because women, particularly alone, did not travel easily like men. With Leach this would present no difficulties. Leach, commissioned to write a book about his visit to Japan[9] and one on the first Kenzan,[10] hoped Janet would type out the manuscripts. In addition Leach, Yanagi, Hamada and Kanjiro Kawai,[11] another highly respected potter, ('the big four' as Janet called them), were planning a book on pottery and needed secretarial assistance. After spending time with Leach, she sensed his loneliness and his need for female company.

The journey, under the auspices of the folk craft movement, took them to, among other places, Kobe, Kyoto, Tamba and the area north of Mashiko. In the heat of August they escaped to the comfort of the luxurious Kazanso Hotel, Matsumoto, to enjoy the cool mountain air and to work on the various manuscripts and books. Hamada, Kawai and Yanagi came to discuss their book on pottery.[12] One afternoon Kawai produced the equipment for the traditional tea ceremony, *mattcha*,[13] and attempted to teach Janet the mannered rituals. It was not a success. He thought she lacked the necessary grace to carry out the movements, deciding that until her 'soul was attuned' her efforts would inevitably not have the required sensitivity and understanding. She subsequently retreated into the more mundane work of typing the chapters of the books Leach was steadily writing.

Far from remaining a purely business arrangement, and despite her lack of sensitivity over the tea ceremony, Leach and Janet spent increasing amounts of time together, often experiencing the pleasure of finding themselves in complete agreement about what they wanted to do. They wandered

ABOVE: Janet Leach – Bottle, coiled and thrown, facted sides, stoneware, 1979, H about 40cm

the hills admiring the grasses and pines of the steep slopes with their orange and pink flowers; they sat and watched the dragonflies and listened to the chirping of the crickets. They soon became close friends and subsequently lovers.

In the seclusion of the mountains they spoke of their past lives, their hopes and ambitions, with Leach confiding the problems of two failed marriages, of the difficulties of running his pottery in St Ives and its future prospects under the care of his eldest son David. He also told her of his long-held desire to settle in Japan, an idea that was beginning to grow in Janet's head. More ominously he told her – someone who distrusted all religions – about the importance of his Bahá'í faith and his difficulty in deciding between whether to continue as a leading potter or commit

ABOVE TOP: Janet Darnell, Tamba, 1954
ABOVE MIDDLE: Kiln firing, Tamba, 1954
ABOVE BOTTOM: Janet Darnell's first pots fired at Tamba

[14] Colloquially known as *benjo*
[15] For a full account see Janet Leach, 'Tamba', *Pottery Quarterly*, vol. 4, no. 13, Spring 1957, pp8-17

his life to working for his belief. Given her knowledge of Leach as a potter and teacher and the respect this commanded, Janet viewed the idea with some scepticism. Encouraged by Leach, who hoped that she would discover its meaning and value, she read about the Bahá'í but remained cautious and uncommitted, though later she became positively hostile.

After the peace and intimacy of the mountain retreat, further travel involved resolving mundane matters such as identifying hotels where they could ensure being able to spend time alone. Staying in traditional Japanese houses, however refined, proved difficult. It was accepted that other residents, curious to see their room, could arrive unannounced. Equally, there was little notion of Western privacy. The toilet[14] arrangements Janet found worryingly primitive. It was not so much that guests were expected to supply their own toilet paper but that the floor hole, usually a long oblong slit some three feet long and one foot wide, she thought far too small. Only in Western-style hotels did they feel safe from inquisitive eyes.

Having established a close and loving relationship they made a tentative plan for their future that involved Leach returning to England, divorcing his second wife from whom he was separated, returning within a year and marrying Janet in Hong Kong before they settled permanently in Japan. Here they hoped to buy a house and set up a pottery. As a first step he gave Janet £500 with a view to purchasing a suitable property near the old capital Kyoto which, apart from being a good distance from Tokyo, had the added attraction for Leach of an active Bahá'í group. It seemed an ideal scheme and following Leach's departure Janet was happy to resume work as a potter secure in the knowledge that her future lay in Japan.

With an awareness that remaining at Mashiko to study was not going to be possible given Hamada's reluctance, Janet accepted his suggestion that it would be better for her to work at a country pottery – where he had learnt – rather than with him. Despite wanting to remain with the man she regarded as her master and mentor she accepted his advice to train elsewhere. The traditional potteries of Okinawa were suggested, as the island would be warmer in the winter months, but having visited the village of Tamba and admiring the austere and, to her eye, authentic pots they produced, and knowing of Hamada's admiration for them, she decided that this was where she would like to be. Ignoring warnings about the bitterly cold winter weather, she came to an agreement with the Ichino family of potters to work with them, studying traditional making and firing techniques while making her own pots. She also hoped to learn Japanese from their children. She arrived in the middle of December 1954, and her initial plan, to stay three months, was extended to six.[15]

Tamba, set in the mountains about seventy kilometres from Osaka and Kyoto, was little more than a hamlet. Bordered by stark triangular mountains 2,000-3,000 feet high, the bleak but powerful landscape offered magnificent views across the twenty-mile long valley running due north and south. The morning sun threw the wooded slopes into dramatic shadow, a spectacle usually accompanied by the song of Japanese nightingales. Its isolated position meant that it had been little visited, even by the American forces.

ABOVE TOP: Janet Darnell at Ichino Pottery, Tamba, 1954

ABOVE BOTTOM: Janet Darnell with Kenkichi Tomimoto, Japan, 1954 (Leach Archive, Crafts Study Centre)

Pottery Heaven | **47**

ABOVE TOP: Ichino family, Tamba, 1954

ABOVE MIDDLE: Washing clothes, Tamba, 1954

ABOVE BOTTOM: Janet Darnell wearing kimono, Japan, 1954

OPPOSITE: Janet Darnell unpacking kiln, Tamba, 1954

[16] Janet Darnell letter, December 1954. P.C.
[17] Ibid.

One of the original *Rokkoyo* (Six Old Kilns of Japan), Tamba had been the site of pot-making for 800 years, with the ware fired in Korean-type kilns. In the mid fifties, before the so-called *Mingei* boom, it still retained much of its traditional character for simply made and decorated wares.

The Ichino family consisted of Toshio Ichino, a small, gentle man in his mid forties, and his wife, in her early thirties, who Janet thought intelligent. She spent much of her time looking up words in Janet's dictionaries in order to ask questions, chiefly about her family, America, and whether she was warm enough. Their two boys aged thirteen and nineteen were friendly and talkative. Also living in the house were grandpa, 'bowlegged and without a tooth in his head who grinned a lot and drank saki at night', and grandma, 'a small bird-like figure with glasses at the end of her nose who cackles and smokes a small pipe'.[16] Toshio was helped by his younger brother Hirouki, who lived in his own house with his wife, son and daughter. Although the Ichino pottery was the largest in Tamba, Hamada had suggested the possibility of working in another potter's workshop, Mr Okuda, but Janet did not like his pots, thinking they borrowed too much from Hamada and did 'not reflect real spirit of Tamba... He is rather tight and meticulous and polishes, measures, polishes, measures, and I have never seen more un-free throwing even in America'.[17]

If working with the Ichinos was deeply rewarding, life in the mountains in winter proved something of a trial, as Hamada had indicated. With no modern forms of lighting, not even battery fuelled flashlights, the modest glow of paper lanterns was the chief form of illumination. In addition, clothes had to be washed by hand in the stream. Doors were never closed and the only warmth came from the *hibache*, the stove filled with glowing charcoal. 'Nothing is heated – one never takes a coat off in Japan – wear the same clothes inside and out... we sit around a huge pot of ashes with a small charcoal fire in the middle', was Janet's bleak description. To deal with the basic living conditions Janet donned extra layers of clothes, managing to stay warm and, to her surprise, free of colds.

The basic diet consisted of different forms of rice occasionally supplemented by wild boar, caught when an

ABOVE: Janet Darnell, Tamba, 1954

animal strayed into the village. Breakfast was traditionally a strong soup made of fermented soya bean curd. On special feast days raw fish was served, which, fortunately, Janet liked, and hence avoided looking like a stuffy foreigner, but large platters of small tit-bits of raw horsemeat, which were dipped in soya and other hot seasonings, she found more of a challenge.

Friends and members of her family in America sent food parcels, which ideally included instant coffee – an essential – and candy, which she liked to nibble. For Christmas, one friend, Mrs Chambers, sent what Janet described as 'a positive feast', the package including butter, jam, bacon, roast beef, chicken, sugar, coffee, nuts and plum pudding plus a huge tinned turkey. This Janet cooked for the Hamada family, managing to brown it by pushing it diagonally into a tiny tin oven that sat over the charcoal burner. Amazingly she was able to make giblet gravy, and the turkey proved to be so tender that they were able to eat it with chopsticks. The family nodded their approval, which surprised Janet as it was so much richer than the usual Japanese diet, though a fruit cake proved too indigestible and she ended up eating this by herself.

ABOVE : Janet Leach – Pot, coiled, thrown and beaten, stoneware, 1979, H about 20cm

Curious to know everything about America, the Ichinos eagerly examined all the packaging on her letters and parcels, cutting off and saving the stamps and demanding to know every detail of her way of life. To demonstrate how Christmas was celebrated in America, Janet decorated a small tree using cigarette foil and any bits of coloured paper she could find, fixing on small candles with clay. It was much enjoyed. For the Japanese New Year the family produced copious amounts of special food, much of which was made from a sticky type of rice that was steamed and pounded in a huge wooden mortar before being rolled into balls. Janet thought it 'like a rather firm wallpaper paste'. Although difficult to consume, in that the balls seemed resistant to chewing, cutting or swallowing, Janet was plied with more. Part of the celebrations involved a special trip to

Pottery Heaven | 51

ABOVE TOP: Kiln, Tamba, 1954

ABOVE BOTTOM: Shinto shrine

OPPOSITE: Janet Leach – Bottle, coiled and thrown, black stoneware, 1980, H about 18cm (Photo: Peter Hoare; Collection: Buckinghamshire County Museum, Aylesbury)

a Shinto shrine where they rang a bell and clapped their hands to attract the gods before bowing with their hands in the prayer position, which they then brought to their forehead and clapped again. Janet found the simplicity of the ceremony strangely moving. Toshio Ichino carried out the same ritual at the pottery shrine before starting work.

In the pottery the small Korean-type wheels proved too small for Janet and a slightly larger one was obtained, which, though still cramped, was manageable. As the flywheel was lighter than the ones she had been used to, she found that to throw it was necessary to use softer clay and more delicate movements while kicking continually with her feet. At first, to adjust to the qualities of the local clay, she learnt to throw small bowls off a large lump, or hump, copying the traditional shapes made at the pottery. The sticky clay, with its low level of plasticity, meant that making handles and spouts was tricky. The larger pots proved even more difficult, for when made by conventional throwing, she discovered that most of the bottoms cracked. This was the reason why the Korean potters first made a base by pressing a ball of clay flat on the wheel, then forming the walls by rolling a length of clay between their hands up in the air to make a coil before attaching it to the base and then throwing it.

The Tamba method of coiling and throwing, especially on larger pots, was the technique that made the biggest impression and was one that Janet continued to practise throughout her life. The added coils were thrown with the help of a piece of stiffish, rough cloth draped inside and out and the clay pulled up into a thin cylinder at one pass. For this the clay was softer than for the usual throwing. As Janet wrote: 'I've tried it and it works'. For bigger forms half or a third of it was thrown and allowed to stiffen before further coils were added. In assessing the traditional pots made at the pottery, Janet thought that 'this place is like apples on a tree – not every one a perfect specimen, but every one has the flavour.'

The kilns were equally intriguing, retaining a basic structure that was thought to have originated in Korea several hundred years earlier. These 'snake kilns' were about 100 feet long, three feet high and five feet wide, built on a slope; about every two feet along the sides were

ABOVE: Janet Darnell, Tamba, 1954

portholes where long pieces of wood were poked in during the firing to fall directly on and around the unglazed pots placed there. These were stacked one on top of each other without the use of shelves, the embers sometimes covering them completely. When the wood and ashes piled up this was prodded down with a long poker; if a pot got upset in the process, the poker was used to put it upright. Firing the kiln evoked a sense of history and tradition that Janet found intensely fulfilling. In these long kilns the stoking path was cross-wise every fourteen inches up the climbing kiln, which gave ample opportunity to put pots where the wood would fall on them. Any embers on the pots were subsequently ground off. Some pots were carefully placed so that one side was exposed to the stoking area to produce a variety of flash marks.

ABOVE: Janet Leach – Lidded pot, coiled and thrown, faceted sides, black stoneware, 1982, H18cm (Photo: Peter Hoare; Collection: Buckinghamshire County Museum, Aylesbury)

In comparison to the life of elegant refinement Janet had experienced in Tokyo and Mashiko, life in Tamba was basic, qualities she saw reflected in the direct and uncomplicated forms of their pots. Only the slip-trailed decoration of delicate, beautifully simplified abstracted motifs of shrimp and chrysanthemum seemed an indulgence. Traditional forms included saki jars that when fired were slung on ropes, looking like a bunch of grapes, to be carried over the mountains.

As a Westerner – *gai-jin*, the foreigner – working in a remote and little known village, Janet was an oddity, her presence attracting a constant stream of visitors, newspaper and newsreel reporters, all of whom insisted on peering over her shoulder as she worked. As one of the few Western women to study pottery in Japan and the only Westerner to

Pottery Heaven | 55

ABOVE: Janet Leach – Bowls, thrown, black stoneware, c1980, H about 7cm

work in Tamba, she, and the work she was doing, were a constant source of amazement. The visitors not only brought an unwelcome reminder of the outside world, a world Janet wanted to escape from – at least for a time – but endlessly disrupted her potting. Many visitors, who had never seen a Westerner before, wanted to see her merely to satisfy their curiosity.

With the initial differences between herself and Richard Hieb sorted out they teamed up to see more of the country potteries, travelling to remote locations by train and bus and, if necessary, they were prepared to walk for miles. Centres visited included Kyushu, Shikoku, Onda and Koishibara, all of which fulfilled their expectations in seeing pots still made by traditional methods. At Arita, where export porcelain had been made for years, they found 'a wonderful old man in an outlying village making water jars about 3ft tall which was like stepping into Korea 100 years ago', such experiences confirming her impression of a country, which, in spite of Westernisation, was still steeped in tradition.

At Tamba, in addition to a full working schedule and what seemed like an endless stream of banal questions from members of the press, there were invitations to speak to various societies, some of which Janet accepted. In long letters to her parents in Texas and friends at Threefold Farm she gave detailed descriptions of life at Tamba. In addition she also wrote accounts about her time in Japan with a view to possible publication. In one piece she explained the American approach to family life, including her own, which, as she pointed out, was in great contrast to the Japanese where love and respect for the extended family never ceased to impress her.[18] In an article, 'Why I Came to Study in Japan', she set out her view of the country expressed in romantic terms with a slightly patronising air that was very much in tune with the ideas put forward by Yanagi and Leach. 'I believe [Japan] to be one of the few remaining places in the world where potters are still living and working in the purity of a natural balance of life and work in a healthy attunement to the East. As pottery is composed of the many elements of the earth, there remains an intuitive awareness of the "Natural Order of Things" which results in the work from these areas being usually

[18] Janet Darnell, 'Impressions of Life in Rural Japan', copy manuscript. n.d. P.C.
[19] Janet Darnell, 'Why I Came to Study in Japan', 1955. P.C.
[20] June 27 – July 2, 1955

ABOVE: Janet Leach – Bottles, thrown, stoneware, c1990, H tallest 22cm (Photo: Jason Wason; Collection: Joanna Wason)

far superior in Spirit to the individually conceived pot of the artist potter. Of course the rural Japanese is not aware of his rich heritage, but this is as it should be.'[19]

Without her knowledge, plans had been made to hold an exhibition of her pots at Osaka Takumi Trading Co, which added to the pressure to produce rather than learn. Feeling unprepared, she managed to delay the show for a few months. The exhibition[20] was to be shared with Richard Hieb, who, she felt, had the advantage of having worked in Japan a year longer than her. Nevertheless, their work was well received and each sold twenty-five pots, producing a useful 2,500 yen. For the final few months of her stay Janet worked at Bizen, on the southern coast of Honshu on the shores of the Inland Sea, where she was again fascinated by the firing methods, which involved stoking the kiln for seven days to achieve the depth of surface and an attractive range of markings that she much admired.

The idyll that Janet experienced working and studying in Japan was reflected in her deepening feelings for Leach

ABOVE: Janet Leach – Bottle, coiled and thrown, poured glaze decoration, red stoneware, 1979, H about 20cm

OPPOSITE: Janet Leach – Bottle, coiled and thrown, poured glaze decoration, stoneware, c1980, H about 30cm

and her wish to marry him and remain in the country. In long, passionate letters she spoke of her love and her longing for them to be together, while often criticising him for what she saw as his inability to change. In return he poured out his feelings about their relationship, what was happening at the Leach Pottery in England, the activities of his family and friends and his deepening conviction that they should marry and settle in Japan.[21] In turn she was often frank and revealing, writing directly about their 'fucking' and lovemaking in a manner that both shocked and delighted him in equal measure. A sharp observer of human behaviour, she related a story about Richard Hieb who, at Hamada's suggestion, had worked with potters on the Okinawa Islands. After living like a native he returned to Mashiko enthusing over the Okinawans whom he saw as so natural and uninhibited that they relieved themselves anywhere, even on the footpaths. 'Got to shit in the path to be a good potter',[22] was Janet's dry and unenthusiastic response. Despite the confessional tone of many of the letters, there was one subject about which Janet chose to remain silent, which was her bisexuality. Given the profound impact on Leach when he subsequently discovered this a few years after they were married, it was a serious omission.

Their plan to settle in Japan was thrown into confusion by two totally unforeseen events, one from David Leach, currently managing the pottery at St Ives, the other from their friends in Japan who began to question the wisdom of Leach moving there permanently. They expressed misgivings about Janet's age – half that of Leach – and about her motives for marrying so eminent a potter. They may also have found her manner too brash and loud. Yanagi feared that the relationship would have a negative effect on Leach's work; he also cited friends who thought Janet was not 'a woman for you',[23] while being vague about the reasons why. Even Hamada was cautious with regard to their relationship. Although he had supported Janet in her endeavour to study and learn in Japan, suspecting that she had hoped for a close friendship with Leach, he had done so probably largely at his friend's request and maintained a distant attitude to her professionally. Janet quickly became

[21] Janet retained many of Leach's airmail letters to her and carbon copies of hers to him
[22] Bernard Leach letter to Mark Tobey, November 28, 1956. P.C.
[23] A letter from Yanagi quoted by Bernard Leach to Janet Darnell, May 22, 1955. P.C.

ABOVE: Janet Leach – Bottle with lug handles, coiled and thrown, black stoneware, c1980, H10cm
(Photo: Peter Kinnear)

[24] David Leach set up the Lowerdown Pottery at Bovey Tracey, south Devon

aware that Hamada, too, believed Leach should remain in England and manage his own pottery, partly because he thought it had lost direction and needed Leach to take a meaningful lead.

Reluctantly, but in the face of such deep-seated opposition, Leach, despite feeling marooned in St Ives, felt he had no alternative but to abandon his intention of moving to Japan with Janet, and that he would have to stay in England. In a major change of plan he suggested that Janet come to St Ives, marry him, and that they would both live and work at the Leach Pottery. Given that their initial intention had been based solely on them settling in Japan, such a drastic change posed a challenging decision for Janet and was not a scheme she at first welcomed. She knew nothing about life in England apart from the difficulties with his family who, he said, tended to regard him as 'a piece of furniture'. Above all she desired to remain in Japan. However, given her feelings for Leach, which were a combination of respect and affection, knowing that her funds were running low and feeling that, after two years in Japan, she now did not wish to return to Threefold Farm, she eventually agreed to Leach's proposal. While professing to love Leach, Janet's feelings were based on a limited knowledge of him, and an assumption that they would start a new life together. He also offered an entrée into the pottery world that would ensure her work was taken seriously.

Challenging though their future plans to live together in St Ives were, even these were thrown into doubt when Leach told his son of his impending marriage and his intention to live in St Ives. Such unexpected news came as a great shock and reversed everything his father had previously agreed, leading David to declare that he could not remain as manager if he had to share the pottery with another potter. Having been given the pottery buildings three years earlier and being charged with managing the business in his father's absence in America and Japan, he had the impression that he was now free to run it in his own way. Such a fundamental change in his father's plans, relegating him again to the role of foreman and manager, was not acceptable and, given the change, he decided that this was the moment to set up on his own. He duly handed in his notice

ABOVE: Janet Leach – Saki set, thrown and turned, finger wipe glaze decoration, stoneware, c1980, H tallest 12cm

with the intention of establishing his own workshop, which he did the following year in south Devon.[24]

David's decisive action posed a dilemma for both Leach and Janet as neither wanted nor planned to run a production pottery; Leach had attempted this following David's departure but felt he was too out of touch to take control, while Janet knew that she had neither the necessary experience nor the desire to take on a managerial role. When they initially agreed to live at St Ives both had assumed David would continue to act as manager, leaving them free to make their own pots. With profound doubts, but a belief that their love could triumph, Janet sailed to England to marry Bernard Leach. She arrived in London the day after his sixty-ninth birthday on January 5, 1956.

5 Manager, Wife, Potter
St Ives 1956-62

ABOVE TOP: St Ives, 1950s

ABOVE BOTTOM: The Leach Pottery

OPPOSITE: Janet Leach working on Leach kick wheel, c1958

[1] Married under the name of Janet Darnell Roland, of Buena Siesta, Upper Stennack, St Ives, her father is named as Charles Walter Darnell, bread company agent, and states that a previous marriage was dissolved. The name Roland remains a mystery

[2] Frances Horne was local philanthropist who had set up the St Ives Handicraft Guild, funding the Leach Pottery for three years

St Ives in 1956 seemed to Janet, despite the lively and progressive art community, even more distant, remote and alien than the mountain village of Tamba. Regardless of its fame as a tourist attraction, the summer season was a mere six weeks when the town filled with tourists, offering local shops and businesses the possibility of making substantial sales. The town, some 300 miles from London, was still a sleepy backwater, where, as Janet was to comment later, avocados were virtually unknown and even grapefruit hard to come by. St Ives must have seemed a forgotten enclave, parochial and distant from the attractions of London, a distance she bewailed, feeling herself by nature a city rather than a country person. Neither the town nor the Leach Pottery had reckoned on the impact of this powerful, ambitious personality who had no inhibitions in stamping her own identity on the town.

The Leach Pottery, established in 1920 by Bernard Leach, assisted by Hamada, stood, surrounded by green fields, on the main Penzance road just outside the town, though within twenty years houses would slowly encroach and eventually surround it. Until their marriage on March 26, 1956 at Penzance Register Office,[1] Janet lodged in a nearby bed and breakfast, Leach arguing that conventions should be respected. Their marriage was witnessed by Leach's eldest daughter Eleanor Nance and by Margery Horne, a family friend and daughter of Frances Horne,[2] the woman who had initially sponsored Leach's move to the town. A three-day honeymoon was spent touring round the Lizard Peninsular in a Hillman car before settling into the handsome but modest property known as Pottery Cottage. At Leach's insistence Janet reluctantly agreed to take part in a Bahá'í wedding ceremony in August during a Bahá'í summer school in Buxton.

62 | Janet Leach: A Potter's Life

ABOVE TOP: Pottery Cottage

ABOVE BOTTOM: Janet Leach – Bottle, coiled and thrown, incised decoration, stoneware, c1974, H about 20cm

OPPOSITE: Janet Leach – Jar with lug handles, coiled and thrown, black stoneware, 1980, H about 15cm (Photo: Peter Kinnear)

Pottery Cottage, which stood immediately adjacent to the pottery workshop, had been built by Leach in the late 1920s, initially intended for pottery workers until it was occupied briefly by his son David when he got married. After the war Leach had lived there with his second wife, Laurie, and their adopted son Maurice. When the marriage failed Leach shared it with students. In anticipation of Janet's arrival, Leach, a great hoarder who rarely threw anything away, had attempted to tidy up, but after the minimalism and simplicity of Japanese houses the cottage seemed to Janet dark and cluttered with objects and furniture. The curtains hung in tatters and her impression was that it desperately needed a thorough overhaul. Despite Leach's sincerity in wanting to create a home for them both, he was reluctant to allow anything to be changed or discarded, thus making it difficult for Janet to feel any sense of ownership or to give the house the imprint of her own personality.

Well aware that 'marriage and a profession make for problems', Janet knew that she faced several challenges, which included building a relationship that was fair and equal while maintaining a measure of her own identity. In the pottery she was aware of the pressure not only to assume managerial responsibility but also to ensure its financially viability. At the same time she had to establish herself as a potter who did not fall into the 'Leach mould'. The pottery had been operating for thirty-five years, during which time it had developed well-established ways of working; its national and growing international reputation for producing high quality ware needed to be maintained and expanded. Following David Leach's departure the 'crew', consisting of experienced, skilled makers along with students and others, lacked positive artistic leadership and direction. Leach had tried to take on this role but felt it beyond his capabilities and, despite Janet's lack of experience, he was only too happy to hand this duty to her.

Although Janet knew that she lacked the ambition to run such a large and busy production workshop she was prepared to accept the responsibility and to do it as professionally as she knew how. Although she had briefly worked in two production potteries and had, for a time, learned to throw some of the forms, her own interest lay solely in

ABOVE: Leach Pottery standard ware, c1960

OPPOSITE: Janet Leach – Vase, coiled and thrown, red stoneware, black and white glaze pattern, 1959, H23cm

making individual pieces, not production ware. The Leach Pottery's range of tableware – Leach standard ware – demanded technical skill and an understanding of forms that Janet was not familiar with, and so she was unable to assess whether they were well or badly made. The pots were sold direct to customers in the pottery showroom, wholesale to shops across the country and through mail order. Many of the processes used were slow and labour-intensive. The preparation of the clay body, for example, was lengthy and time-consuming, while the large, oil-fired three-chamber kiln needed at least five days of skilled attention to ensure success; however, although noisy and smelly, it produced good results.

Alongside the standard ware, which Leach had designed but never made, he produced individual pieces bearing his personal stamp. These included bottles, lidded pots, plates, bottles, bowls and dishes in stoneware and porcelain, which he made either alone or, for the larger pieces, with the help of a skilled potter. In theory his pieces had pride of place in the kiln, positioned to suit the form and glaze to obtain the best results.[3] Leach's pots were an important part of production in contributing to the pottery's financial viability, an aspect Janet quickly recognised and sought to expand. Any good but flawed pieces that emerged from the kiln were often given to Janet as presents on special occasions such as Christmas or her birthday. Over the years she slowly built up a collection of fine wares that eventually formed part of the Leach Museum at the pottery.[4]

It was a convention that workers at the pottery were encouraged to make individual pots in their own time that were then offered for sale in the showroom, with them getting a proportion of the selling price. This aspect of production, Janet felt, could be given greater significance in bringing in a different and welcome element to the showroom and she was appalled to discover that the potters were only allowed to put up one or two pieces no larger than a small casserole dish in each firing. She duly increased this number, realising that this encouraged them to develop their own ideas.

At Mashiko and Tamba, Janet had been deeply impressed by the quiet, relaxed industry and harmonious atmosphere, which she described as 'pottery heaven'. Such tranquillity

[3] Occasionally Janet found that Leach's pots had not been given precedence and remonstrated with the kiln packers, insisting that they place them first
[4] This collection was handed over to the Crafts Study Centre, Farnham (which houses the Leach Archives), by the Redgrave estate in lieu of tax and will be on show at the Leach Pottery when it opens after restoration (2007)

ABOVE: Janet Leach – Bottle, hand-built, porcelain, c1965, H17cm (Collection: Camberwell College of Arts, University of the Arts London)

seemed absent from St Ives where, despite the sleepy atmosphere of the town, the pottery was competing to sell its wares in a small, specialised market. In addition there were also many personal rivalries and power struggles, though the skills of the potters was unquestionably high.

Many were ex-apprentices, mostly Cornish, with no previous art education. 'They were proud of their abilities and successes with the high level of the standard-ware... Pottery for Use was the motto', wrote Janet, adding that privately she referred to it as 'a stewpot psychology'.[5] The crew was led by William (Bill) Marshall, an able and respected maker, who had arrived as a youth in 1938. After serving an apprenticeship, apart from war service, he remained at the pottery, becoming a key worker producing well-thrown standard ware as well as his individual forms. Marshall, who helped teach the apprentices and students, was also responsible for maintaining the quality of the ware, and he worked with Leach on his larger pieces. The team included ex-apprentices Scott Marshall, who was Marshall's cousin, Richard Batterham and Dinah Dunn, together with students. Other crew members included Horatio Dunn and Joe Binney who mixed clay, packed and sent off pots and helped fire the kiln, while Frank Vibert kept the accounts and served as a general business manager. In all there were some ten workers who had to be dealt with and directed.

Taking over the management was an unenviable task for an inexperienced newcomer who had not only to deal with a natural resistance to an outsider, but who, however unwittingly, was seen as being responsible for David Leach's departure. As the wife of Bernard Leach she was also in a privileged position, seen to carry some of his authority without yet having earned it. Determined to manage, Janet brought her organisational skills to bear. Having successfully set up and run a pottery in a hospital for three years, opened her own workshop in New York State and raised funds to go to Japan, it was evident that, whatever her inexperience in running a production workshop, she had a sound aptitude for organisation.

After sorting out the office to her liking she had to discover how the production system operated, a task made more difficult as the advice she received was often contradictory.

[5] Janet Leach, 'Fifty One Years of the Leach Pottery', *Ceramic Review*, no. 14 March/April 1972, pp4-7

ABOVE: Janet Leach – Dishes, hand-built, poured glaze, stoneware, c1985, L about 15cm

Furthermore, even basic information could be elusive. The size guides for the standard ware, with the weights of clay and thrown measurements for each item, were unaccountably missing. Undeterred, the guides were redrawn and the sizes established. Each week it was Janet's responsibility to issue a 'make list' of items included in the catalogue that were required to fulfil orders and replenish stock as well as suit the packing requirements of the kiln. This involved keeping a close eye on the order book, an understanding of the complexity of making each piece and what a thrower could be reasonably expected to make in a week. With only limited experience of repetition throwing she was initially misled as to the number of items it was reasonable for a potter to throw in a day with the result that, at first, Janet's lists tended to be light rather than demanding. Paradoxically, while this meant a more relaxed working day, such a change was not always welcomed by the throwers who wanted the pottery to succeed, and, as they were paid bonus payments,

fewer pots meant less money. The amounts were soon increased to more appropriate quantities.

As a matter of principle Janet tried to ensure that over the period of two years students would try out all the shapes, not just the ones they found easy, yet she spotted what each potter was best at and sought to match shape to character. When Gwyn John (later Gwyn Hanssen Pigott), an able potter who had trained with Ivan McMeekin in Australia, found beer tankards difficult she was given smaller, more meticulous items such as soup bowls and mugs, at which she excelled. With John Reeve, another careful potter, a useful collaboration was set up whereby, on lidded pots, he threw the bases while she produced the lids. So precisely were each of the parts made that they fitted perfectly. Richard Jenkins proved adept at throwing porcelain.

Despite her lack of experience, Janet soon saw that changes and improvements could be beneficial. From working in Tamba, where potters used and relished the qualities of local clay bodies, both she and Leach felt that the regular stoneware body not only lacked character – she described it as being 'like window putty' – but also involved lengthy, labour-intensive production, a process she thought could be shortened. Eventually a seam of attractively textured stoneware clay was located on a farm owned by Joe Dobble in the nearby village of St Agnes, which, when used pretty much as dug, was combined half and half with other clays to become the standard body.

ABOVE TOP: Janet Leach – Bottle, stoneware, slab built, incised and painted decoration, c1965, H38cm (Collection: Cornwall County Council)

ABOVE BOTTOM: Janet Leach working on Leach kick wheel, c1958

OPPOSITE: Janet Leach – Bottle, coiled and thrown, poured glaze, black stoneware, c1980, H18cm (Photo: David Westwood; Collection: Crafts Study Centre)

Some shapes were also adjusted. As an able cook and housekeeper who was expected to cater for Leach and, on occasion, entertain visitors, Janet soon found some items of standard ware needed redesigning. The plates, she declared, were 'too mean' and were duly made larger; a soup jug was abandoned as being no longer suited to modern life and the stewpot, which stood on a narrow base, was described as 'impractical' after Janet discovered that the juice stayed at the bottom, leaving the other contents to dry out at the top. It was given a wider base. She also persuaded Leach to design a range of different sized all-purpose jugs. To adapt to the changing times the working day was later re-timed to begin at nine rather than eight, a part of Janet's reorganisation that went down well.

ABOVE: Janet Leach with Atsuya Hamada, 1960s (Leach Archive, Crafts Study Centre)

OPPOSITE PAGE: Janet Leach – Bottle, coiled and thrown, poured glaze, black stoneware, c1980, H about 42cm (Photo: David Westwood; Collection: Crafts Study Centre)

[6] Richard Batterham and Dinah Dunn were married shortly after and set up a pottery in Dorset

[7] Quick was an amusing and lively worker who lived in St Ives; his partner, Norman Stocker, a car mechanic, who had a wooden leg, sometimes worked for Barbara Hepworth

Introducing change to the working methods almost inevitably met with opposition, which highlighted personality differences. Perhaps in an attempt to cover up her uncertainty and inexperience, Janet could be aggressive and argumentative. After a series of disagreements, Frank Vibert, the manager/bookkeeper, left, as did Dinah Dunn, a skilled thrower who had been helping devise a new, more translucent porcelain body. Richard Batterham, a promising student who had studied pottery at Bryanston School, followed her.[6] Others took their place but the climate of students wanting to train as potters was changing. The introduction of well-funded and broadly based ceramic courses at art schools and generously funded grants meant that many would-be students shied away from the more disciplined and directed workshop training. To boost the number of trained potters, Kenneth Quick, who had been an apprentice and had left to set up his own pottery in the town, was persuaded to return. Talented, adept and amusing, he was seen as a future manager, a plan brought to an end with his tragic death in a swimming accident in Japan in 1961.[7]

ABOVE: Janet Leach working on Leach kick wheel, c1958

OPPOSITE: Janet Leach – Bowl, thrown, faceted red stoneware, 1959, H17cm (Photo: Peter Hoare; Collection: Buckinghamshire County Museum, Aylesbury)

[8] b.1935. Gwyn John planned to marry her Australian fiancé at St Ives, all preparations were made, Janet baked a cake, but on the wedding eve Gwyn cancelled the wedding and subsequently married Louis Hanssen, who later became a potter. See The Studio Potter, vol. 19, no. 8, December 1991, pp46-50
[9] 1929-86, Leach Pottery 1957-58
[10] b.1929. Paid a wage of £2, 10s, 0d (£2.50) a week
[11] 1933-2002
[12] b.1935, Leach Pottery 1962-63
[13] b.1939, Leach Pottery 1963-65
[14] This technique had been practised at the pottery since the twenties, but his skill enabled much larger pieces to be produced

In the light of the changes in art school education, Janet proposed that the policy of taking apprentices be dropped in favour of accepting 'student apprentices' to supplement the work of the core potters. The assistants, mostly students from overseas, often came with government funding on a one- or two-year work trainee basis. In the mid and late fifties these included Len Castle and Peter Stichbury from New Zealand, Anna Kjaersgaard from Denmark, Gwyn John,[8] Nurmala Pandit from India, Hamada's son Atsuya,[9] Helena da Silva from South America, Pierre Culot from Belgium and John Reeve,[10] a French Canadian who came with his heavily pregnant partner, Donna Balma. Reeve and Balma, together with Byron Temple[11] from the United States, who arrived in 1961, Glenn Lewis[12] from Canada, who came a year later followed by Michael Henry,[13] were especially welcomed by Janet as fellow North Americans. English assistants included Derek Emms, Alan Brough, Harry Isaacs and Robin Welch.

The students brought a variety of individual skills and a range of experience. Atsuya Hamada, an expert mould maker, suggested that some of the individual pots could be produced in a mould and then finished and decorated by Leach.[14] One such item was a tall squared bottle, some seventeen to eighteen inches (thirty-five to forty centimetres) high, the model made from one of Leach's thrown forms beaten into a square shape. Once the body was cast a neck was thrown and added and the bottle was covered with a temmoku glaze and decorated by Leach. The fact that such large pieces needed only Leach's finishing touch helped increase the output of his individual pieces, much to Janet's satisfaction.

The days for Janet soon fell into a familiar pattern. The mornings involved sorting out the pottery, attending to correspondence, organising shopping and preparing lunch. In the afternoon, when Leach usually took a nap, Janet made her own pots. Supper was planned in advance with Janet devising a variety of casseroles that could safely be left in the oven, some hot and spicy reflecting her Texan background. Both she and Leach smoked heavily and drank a little wine, though Janet preferred whisky mixed with water, a habit that could occasionally get out of hand. Her heavy smoking left her with a terrible cough, which could

ABOVE: Janet Leach – Bottle, thrown, wood-fired, stoneware, c1980, H about 14cm (Photo: Peter Kinnear)

OPPOSITE: Janet Leach – Bottle, coiled and thrown, black stoneware, 1975, H26cm (Photo: Peter Hoare; Collection: Buckinghamshire County Museum, Aylesbury)

[15] Donna Balma, unpublished autobiographical account
[16] December 27, 1957 – January 3, 1958. The week also included visits to the collection of Sir Alan and Lady Barlow at their arts and crafts-style house Boswells, near Wendover, in the Chilterns, and the British Museum
[17] b1925. Potter and editor of *Crafts Review* and *Pottery Quarterly*
[18] 1902-1985, Leach's first apprentice, was then working as a pottery officer in Nigeria, though he still had his pottery in Wenford Bridge, Cornwall

be terrifying to hear and which, on one occasion, resulted in cracked ribs. With too much whisky her voice lost its ring of natural sincerity and took 'on a conspiratorial edge and gradually slurred its way south until she sounded like a tough, Texan pioneer woman'.[15]

In the evenings, students were often entertained with supper in the cottage when one of the treats was to select any of the pots in the kitchen, whether peasant ware from China or pieces by Leach or Hamada, from which to eat the meal. This, Janet insisted, was part of a commitment to making use of pots that were intended to be functional and enjoyed. During the course of the evening Leach spoke about his early life in Japan, his two visits to Korea and his approach to making pots, but Janet preferred practical topics such as American politics, pottery and shop business accompanied by strong fresh coffee – brewed to her own recipe that, mysteriously, included the use of egg shells – endless cigarettes and Johnnie Walker Red Label whisky. For their first Christmas, just as Janet had improvised a Christmas tree in Tamba, she adorned a twisted bough of blackthorn with silver and decorated it with red candles. As a present Leach gave Janet one of his pots, the first of many. Eleanor and Dicon Nance, Leach's eldest daughter and son-in-law, returned from Thailand and they all attended the midnight service at the parish church.

A full programme in 1957 was typical of their busy schedule. This included a one-week potters' seminar at Pendley Manor,[16] just outside London, organised by Murray Fieldhouse[17] where, among other topics, Leach talked about Zen, tea and pottery and Janet spoke on her time at Tamba and Mashiko. During leave from Nigeria, Michael Cardew[18] held a geology course for potters at his pottery at Wenford Bridge, Cornwall, in September, attended by John Reeve and Janet. Part of the course involved tramping over the Cornish countryside searching for particular types of rocks and minerals, which Janet greatly enjoyed as it tied in with her interest in, and use of, natural materials. Slowly, Janet settled into the rhythm of the pottery and learnt to deal with Leach's likes and dislikes. Although there were often disagreements between them, they both wanted the pottery – and the marriage – to succeed.

ABOVE TOP: Janet Leach – Bottle with splashed glaze pattern, stoneware, 1959, H38cm

ABOVE BOTTOM: Janet Leach – Bottle, thrown, incised decoration, glaze over slip, c1962, H15cm

A Potter of Some Consequence

Despite her attempts to organise the schedule at the pottery, it was often difficult to find time to make her own pots. Burdened with what seemed like endless amounts of administration, Janet felt it important to set up part of the workshop where she could work free from endless questions. Resolutely independent, she was insistent on working separately from Leach, rejecting his offer to have a wheel in his upstairs room, which would have ensured some privacy, preferring instead to clear a corner of the downstairs communal workshop as her own space. While she admired Leach's pots, describing them as coming 'out to meet you... like dancers, they perform for you, they are visually decorative and, of course, not only decorative',[19] it was Hamada she saw as her *sensei* or master. At no time did she see herself as part of 'the Leach tradition'[20] or wish to follow in his footsteps, either in making pots in a similar style or in the forms and techniques she used.

For Janet, the ability to respond spontaneously to the pot as it grew, whether while working on the wheel or building with slabs, was vital. Taking traditional forms she echoed the American potter Jill Bonovitz's view in seeking to imbue the pot 'with my evolving consciousness of my inner self... presenting the vessel with a relaxed yet suspenseful attitude'.[21] Many of her thrown and coiled pots resulted in an organic-like asymmetry that was the result of careful control with an easy, relaxed 'suspenseful' approach. In common with the potter Bill Newland, she thought that throwing was 'concerned with inner force – dynamic growth from the wheel'.[22] Like Leach, she adopted Japanese throwing techniques, which meant that she was a 'clean' potter, using only a minimal amount of water or thin slip with little splashing, so that she got off the wheel as unsoiled as when she got on. During a demonstration to a group of students she pointed out that her white watchstrap was as clay-free after as before throwing. Photographs of Janet sitting at the wheel, working on a large pot, show her without any splashes of clay.[23]

The early shapes she made were a blend of her own ideas, evolved directly out of her experiences in Japan and, despite her protests about rejecting any influence from Leach, some of the lidded jars showed some similarity to the pots that

[19] Quoted in J P Hodin, 'Janet Darnell Leach', *Pottery Quarterly*, vol. 9, no. 33, Autumn 1967, p11
[20] This was a term Janet greatly disliked, suspecting that commentators saw her in such a role
[21] Quoted in Peter Dormer, *The New Ceramics: Trends + Traditions*, Thames and Hudson, London, 1986, p27
[22] *Ibid.*, p33
[23] One such is illustrated in Janet Leach, 'A Potter's Day', *Ceramic Review*, no. 146, March/April 1994, p58

ABOVE LEFT: Janet Leach – Bottle, thrown, stoneware, c1960, H16cm (Collection: Camberwell College of Arts, University of the Arts London)

ABOVE RIGHT: Janet Leach – Bottle, thrown, stoneware, c1960, H18cm (Collection: Camberwell College of Arts, University of the Arts London)

were made at the pottery at the time. Her glazes tended to be those in use at the pottery, though they were often applied one over the other to result in luscious surface qualities. While reflecting influences from the pottery in her early work, in refusing to learn how to throw standard ware and establishing her own space, Janet was adamant in developing her own style and did not welcome what she perceived as interference from Leach. When she became aware of him hovering about to give advice while she was working she would tell him in no uncertain terms to go away. 'Don't you want my criticism?' he would ask, to which 'no' was the emphatic reply, 'not until the pot is finished and fired'.

A series of photographs taken in the late 1950s show Janet at work on a Leach kick wheel and some of the pots she made. Later, she preferred to use a Japanese wheel which was more suited to the larger rounded forms that she started to make. The early thrown shapes included a variety of lidded containers and bottles that were ovoid in shape with narrow necks and distinct throwing rings highlighted by a matt white glaze. Some were decorated in earth-coloured browns and greys with patchwork-like patterns that echoed the landscape of organised fields of rice paddies. In the grid-like structure the ordered surface arrangements combine a

ABOVE TOP: Janet Leach – Bottle, coiled and thrown, poured slip decoration, red stoneware, 1979, H about 40cm

ABOVE BOTTOM: Janet Leach – Bottle, coiled and thrown, stoneware, finger wipe decoration through glaze, c1985, H26cm

OPPOSITE: Janet Leach – Bottle, hand-built, porcelain, 1980, H20cm (Photo: Peter Hoare; Collection: Buckinghamshire County Museum, Aylesbury)

[24] Janet Leach, 'Fifty One Years of the Leach Pottery', *Ceramic Review*, no. 14, March/April 1972, pp4-7

feeling for organic form with a well-thought-out, designed pattern. At this point her style was still evolving, for although she had been in Japan for nearly two years, only a year of that was actually spent making pots.

Such a relaxed, organic approach in terms of form and decoration had little in common with Leach's more symmetrical shapes and florally based abstract decoration, but gradually even the relative order of Janet's early pieces gave way to shapes and surfaces with a more fully integrated feel, with many of her pots celebrating slightly asymmetrical shapes. For the rounded pots her preferred method was throwing on the wheel using a variation of the Japanese coil and throw technique, ideally a process suited to a wheel that enabled her to straddle and lean over the pot. Like many other potters and sculptors, Janet believed that the act of making should involve the maker's body as well as the mind. Such an intimate and physical working relationship between body and machine enabled her to establish a close interaction between the making process and her own body, which allowed her to explore the softness of the shape and the flowing roundness of the form.

Finding even the new standard body too refined and bland, Janet constantly experimented with different clay bodies, using the various textures and colours to evoke mood and intensity. 'The clay body is a major inspiration for my pots',[24] she insisted. At different times the bodies she used included a red sandy brown and a dark black. The addition to the standard body of bauxite, an impure form of aluminium containing iron, resulted in a warm red-brown coloured body when fired, which was usually used for the rounded forms. To produce a black body, ground chrome ore, a refractory material, together with manganese dioxide, were added, the chrome ore preventing the body from bloating or blistering at high temperatures. Technically, the black body was quite an achievement in obtaining a smooth, intense black with a soft silky surface that could withstand the high-temperature reduction firing. The blackness produced a dramatic effect that Janet handled with great sensitivity.

Liking the whiteness of porcelain as a contrast to stoneware, in preference to the smoothness of the usual porcelain body in use at the pottery, Janet devised her own

ABOVE TOP: Shoji Hamada – Dish, thrown, trailed decoration, stoneware, c1980, Ø about 22cm

ABOVE BOTTOM: Hamada glazing a pot, Mashiko, 1954

[25] A trade name of pure china clay grog, supplied in different sizes from dust to coarse
[26] Jonathan Sidney, 'Janet Leach – New Pots', *Ceramic Review*, no. 82, July/August 1983, pp30-31
[27] W A Ismay, 'Pottery by Janet Leach', Southover Gallery, Lewes, February 1981, *Crafts*, no. 50, May/June 1981, pp51-52

variation by wedging in coarse white Molochite.[25] As an admirer of Leach's 'wonderfully delicate thrown porcelains', Janet had no desire to compete with these but nevertheless wanted to make use of the white qualities of the body. The mixture she devised was too rough for throwing and could only be hand-built. When fired, the grog, while forming an integral part of the body, was clearly visible, giving a textural quality that gave the impression of bones breaking through the delicate skin. Often finished with a pale blue celadon glaze and a slash of thin black trails, such pieces seem to encompass movement and action, and, by contrast, ruggedness and refinement. As one reviewer observed: 'when, in some of the pieces, all the processes are pushed to their limit, when movement and stability, control and flamboyance are combined the result is breathtaking'.[26]

Preferring to concentrate on the form of her pieces rather than on elaborate decoration, Janet adopted a broad, minimal approach to surface treatment. For some pieces she made use of the graining on a length of wood to beat or paddle the surface of pots, giving a subtle, incidental surface texture. Other devices included the use of runny textured glazes that complemented the organic feel of the rounded shapes, or a technique she adapted of pouring slashes of glaze. This method, used extensively by Hamada for slip-trailed decoration, Janet interpreted for use with glaze. Using a chipped ladle that 'leaked', with a smooth, assured circular motion Hamada poured a line of thick glaze in a loop-like shape on the top of other glazes, usually on flat dishes rather than on rounded forms, repeating the movement to create a double loop pattern that set up a tension between the flow of the lines and the shape of the dish. The relaxed movement, often repeated on dozens of pots, allowed the easy movement of his arm and pour of the glaze to determine the flowing lines of the pattern formed. Without seeking to replicate Hamada's patterns, Janet, with assured bravado, poured a single slash of glaze on the side of a pot or a dish, sometimes onto the raw clay body, sometimes over another glaze, in a gesture that signified the direct hand of the potter. Commenting on the success of the poured decoration, the critic and collector W A Ismay wrote that to 'pour a glaze pattern with such bold decision down both sides of an

ABOVE: Janet Leach – Bottle, coiled, thrown and beaten, stoneware, 1979, H about 25cm

upright form, or across a broad dish, needs a good eye and co-ordinated abilities of relaxed movement'.[27]

While, paradoxically, adding a disruptive quality to the overall composition, the gash of colour also introduced an element of surprise, highlighting and uniting form and surface. Such an intervention could be seen to echo the action of a Zen master who might shout at or even hit a pupil during meditation to bring them out of mundane life and into enlightenment. To Janet, such interventions on the pots animated the form, adding a discordant but appropriate element of difference. This suggestion of rebellion, while disturbing any easy sense of harmony, added to the tension

ABOVE: Janet Leach – Dish, coiled and thrown, stoneware, 1979, Ø about 45cm

[28] Ian Auld, 'The Leach Pottery 1977', March 11 – April 12, Amalgam Gallery, London, *Crafts*, no. 26, May/June 1977, p46
[29] Others included Heal's, which tended to be unreliable and uneven in the work on display, Wollands, Liberty and the Craft Centre of Great Britain
[30] October 14-24, 1959
[31] Bernard Leach, *Beyond East and West*, Faber and Faber, London, 1978, p258
[32] 1903-1975
[33] Some years ago, when looking through the stores of Manchester City Art Gallery (now Manchester Art Gallery) a tall slab vase was credited to Bernard Leach when it clearly was made by Janet, presumably on the assumption that the handsome piece from the Leach Pottery could only be the work of the great master. This error has now been rectified

within the overall concept of the pot, giving it added life and energy. It was a decorative technique admired by one reviewer as a 'coffee-coloured body harmonised with the rich pourings of dark glaze', who went on to observe that 'Janet Leach is a potter of some consequence'; her pots did not need justifying 'with wordy intellectualising', but had an enviable 'directness'.[28]

In addition to selling her individual pieces in the Leach showroom, an important outlet was Primavera, Henry Rothschild's shop and gallery in Sloane Street, London, one of the small number of quality galleries showing craft in the capital.[29] Rothschild had set up Primavera in the late 1940s to show the best of handmade work from this country and abroad. The gallery had acquired a reputation for high quality craft, particularly that by leading British makers. It also showed a range of handcrafts from countries such as India and Mexico. To select work Rothschild travelled round the country, meeting and talking to makers, including visits to St Ives. As an early supporter of Janet's work, Primavera regularly had her work on the shelves. The gallery was a Mecca for museums and galleries wanting to acquire contemporary craft and most of the early pieces of Janet's work in national collections were purchased there.

The first significant public recognition of her work in Britain came when Rothschild invited her to share an exhibition with William Marshall after only three years working in England.[30] Although the two potters did not always see eye to eye about how the pottery should be run, the fact that they agreed to take part suggests that, professionally, they had respect for each other's work. At this and later shows, Leach was in the position of having to acknowledge publicly Janet's artistic independence. While he may, originally, have assumed his ideas would have a significant influence on her pots, this was not how Janet saw her work developing and she was determined to evolve her own style. Leach described Janet's work as showing 'no direct influence from mine' and having 'great force of character',[31] but the pots were never sufficiently in the 'Leach mould' to allow him to admire them wholeheartedly.

It was symptomatic of the tensions within the relationship between Janet and Leach that there was disagreement over

ABOVE: Janet Leach – Dish, coiled and thrown, poured glaze decoration, stoneware, c1980, Ø about 45cm

what name she should use professionally. As part of their marriage, Janet accepted the convention that she take the name Leach, but had not intended to use this as her professional name, planning instead to retain her maiden name for her work. When this issue was raised with Leach he demanded to know why her married name was not good enough. However much she resisted he insisted, pointing out that conventionally women automatically took the husband's name, completely ignoring the experience of his friend and neighbour, the renowned sculptor Barbara Hepworth.[32] Although married twice, she had retained her maiden name throughout. Somewhat uncharacteristically Janet agreed on a compromise – Janet Darnell Leach – realising that this carried a risk in identifying her closely with Leach and the ideas he represented. At the same time she saw that the name Leach would ensure that her pots would be given serious consideration.[33]

Throughout her professional life Janet remained sensitive to the issue of her artistic independence, about which she

ABOVE: Janet Leach – Lidded pot, coiled and thrown, poured glaze, stoneware, 1979, H about 12cm

had strong feelings, as Tony Ford, then Director of the Crafts Council, was to discover when he made an innocent but sympathetic point about the difficulties of finding time to make pots. In her stinging reply she said 'I am a compulsive potter and have always made pots, even under trying circumstances... I have always refused to exhibit with my husband and my connections in England and Japan have as a matter of principle, always been independent.'[34] In this she was correct, only rarely showing her pots in mixed exhibitions that included Leach's work, but the question of why she worked under the name of Leach remains a matter of speculation.

The Partnership

Quite apart from their professional differences, there were problems from the start of Janet's marriage to Leach over what each expected from the other. Having come to know each other in Japan where they were both at ease and planning a new future, each of them was very different. In Japan Janet experienced Leach as warm, open, amusing and relaxed, in great contrast to his behaviour on his home territory where Janet found him stiff, formal and reluctant to review or question long-established habits. Janet, meanwhile, had been compliant and agreeable in Japan, more than willing to take a secretarial and supportive role, but in Britain as wife and pottery manager she became argumentative and assertive. Despite Leach expressing a willingness to change she felt that he really wanted a conventional marriage with a wife who would look after him unconditionally. There was also the issue of her bisexuality. Having had love affairs with both men and women, Janet declared on one occasion 'I don't know what I am'.

From the tone and passion of their correspondence when he was in St Ives and she in Japan it is clear that she looked for, and he promised, a partnership of professional and emotional equality. In Japan Leach had been willing to think about the way he ran his life and looked forward to setting up a home together there with shared responsibility. By agreeing to the change in plan and to settle in England Janet discovered that not only did she have to run a pottery that had been established for nearly forty years but also to live in a house that had been Leach's home for nearly twen-

[34] Janet Leach to Tony Ford, November 17, 1980 (Janet Leach Archive, Crafts Study Centre)

ABOVE: Janet Leach – Lidded pot, coiled and thrown, faceted sides, stoneware, 1979, H about 11cm

ty years. All of which tended to made profound change difficult. In many ways Janet was a 'modern' woman who had sought to establish her independence from an early age; by contrast, Leach, nearly thirty years older, had a far more traditional view of marriage.

Many of their disagreements, while centring around their domestic arrangements, were, in different ways, tussles for power. He, used to handing out orders, first expected Janet to take responsibility for running their home then, in her view, was unable to leave her to manage it, constantly interfering, suggesting menus and presenting shopping lists of what she should buy. Leach seemed to be comparing the way she ran the home to with how it had been organised before. Not surprisingly, she resented what she saw as Leach's meddling in areas that were her responsibility.

ABOVE TOP: Janet Leach – Bottle, coiled, thrown and beaten, stoneware, 1979, H about 25cm

ABOVE BOTTOM: Janet Leach – Bottle, coiled and thrown, incised decoration, stoneware, 1979, H about 20cm

OPPOSITE: Janet Leach – Bottle, coiled and thrown, stoneware, 1980, H19cm (Photo: Phil Rogers; Collection: Phil Rogers)

When shopping, for example, she preferred to see what was seasonally available and this led to further disagreement. There were also endless quarrels about what she saw as his reluctance to fully acknowledge their marriage, exacerbated by Leach refusing or forgetting to include Janet in his social engagements. From her point of view he had the irritating habit of writing out details of what he felt was going wrong in their relationship while she preferred to discuss and argue, hopefully to resolve any problems. Outspoken and articulate, she was fearless in stating her disquiet and often brutally frank in her criticism of his behaviour.

A further grievance for Janet was Leach's increasing commitment to the Bahá'í faith. This, she felt, took him away from his true vocation, which she saw as making pots. Not only did she totally believe in Leach as an important potter but she also recognised that as he became more established the demand for his work was increasing and that more pieces were required. This, she saw, was good for his reputation and the finances of the pottery. Despite having agreed to attend a Bahá'í Summer School and take part in a Bahá'í wedding, she declined any further involvement or to show interest in the faith, viewing the followers as proselytisers forever trying to secure converts.

The art community in the town offered an outlet for lively and stimulating company, with a regular series of visitors bringing news of London and national activities. Although the number of professional artists at work in and around the town was relatively small, there were powerful progressive elements that offered opportunities for discussion of current issues and the exchange of ideas. Until Ben Nicholson left in the early fifties, he and Barbara Hepworth – dubbed 'the king and queen of St Ives' – were seen as natural leaders. By the late 1950s the community had become more diverse, riven by different factions, though the Penwith Gallery, which promoted the work of artists based in the area whether painting, sculpting, print-making, potting or working in other crafts, remained at its centre. After early struggles to settle disagreements between representational and non-representational art and between fine and applied art, the Penwith was a dynamic and active centre of radical ideas. By the mid fifties the Arts Council

ABOVE: Janet Leach throwing a bowl off hump, c1970

was funding a full-time curator and the galley was showing some of the most adventurous art in the country. Janet later became involved in its organisation, helping to ensure that craft was not neglected or underplayed.

Major artists living in and around the town included Patrick Heron, who was rapidly gaining a reputation for his abstract compositions and respect for his trenchant art criticism that included enthusiastic support for abstract expressionism. During the war, as a conscientious objector, Heron had worked at the Leach Pottery, where he met his future wife, Delia Reiss, but he was critical of Leach for turning his back on industrial production. A skilled mimic, Heron performed sharply observed imitations of Leach, capturing his mannerisms to the amusement of all. Peter Lanyon, Roger Hilton, Wilhelmina Barnes-Graham and William Redgrave, together with many younger painters, also lived in the town, many of whom were regular visitors to the pottery.

Despite the apparent harmony there were deep differences within the art community, not only around the question of abstraction but jealousies of individual success. Such issues were heightened when the flamboyant and irrepressible artist Francis Bacon settled briefly in the town. Disliking Heron's abstract paintings and always outspoken, he dubbed him the Prince of Colour, dismissing his work as having little content. Bacon took a lease on Porthmeor Studios, renting the space from William Redgrave, an artist who ran a small painting school. However, St Ives proved too remote and parochial for Bacon and his stay was not permanent, but he made a great impression.

Not surprisingly, Bacon's figurative and often violent compositions were intensely disliked by, amongst others, Heron, but this did little to deter the energetic and rebarbative artist. Bacon, continuing to paint the figure, persuaded Redgrave's wife, Mary, generally known as Boots, to pose in the nude and he completed several studies of her. By this time Boots had become a great friend of Janet's and Bacon became a regular visitor to the pottery. Despite his declared intention of producing sculpture, there is no record of him working with clay.[35]

As part of establishing her own financial and social independence Janet set up a craft shop in Fore Street in the

[35] For a full account see Martin Harrison, *In Camera*, Thames and Hudson, London, 2004
[36] With David Leach no longer involved, Robert Nance opened a shop on the sea front

ABOVE: Janet Leach – Dish, coiled and thrown, poured glaze decoration, stoneware, c1980, Ø about 20cm

centre of the town, taking over premises that had been run by David Leach and Robert Nance.[36] When this property proved to be in a poor condition, in partnership with Boots Redgrave, she opened a shop at the other end of Fore Street, now called the New Craftsman, selling high quality craft and painting. They also planned a number of other schemes including buying Leach's pots at auction and selling them abroad. Janet also acquired a property, Anchor House, in order to offer accommodation to students. Finding reasonably priced rooms was difficult, especially as she wanted to attract more students from overseas and being able to offer somewhere secure and reasonably priced to live was an added incentive. She also formed her own circle of friends quite apart from those shared with Leach, among whom were Boots, the sculptor John Milne and Barbara Hepworth. Her relationship with Boots was as professional as it was emotional, though some idea of her great admiration for, and liking of, Boots, is suggested in a letter that she later wrote, confessed to having 'started courting your friendship when

ABOVE TOP: Barbara Hepworth (Photo: Irene Winsby)

ABOVE BOTTOM: Bernard Leach and Janet Leach, New York, 1960 (Leach Archive, Crafts Study Centre)

[37] Letter to Mary Redgrave. n.d. (Janet Leach Archive, Crafts Study Centre)
[38] While Leach admired Hepworth's drawings he had little time for her work as a sculptor; on one occasion he was observed leaning against one of her large sculptures while smoking a cigarette and talking endlessly about Japan
[39] This was carved in lignum vitae and is in the collection of the Museum of Modern Art, New York
[40] Quoted in Gerry Williams, 'Janet Leach: American Foreigner', *The Studio Potter*, vol. 11, no. 2, June 1983, pp76-93
[41] Untitled document (Janet Leach Archive, Crafts Study Centre)
[42] 1960
[43] Janet Leach to Bernard Leach, January 12, 1955. P.C.

I'd only been in St Ives 6 months'.[37] They maintained their friendship throughout their lives.

Although Leach was friendly with Hepworth, often dropping into her studio for tea and a gossip about the latest news in the town, Janet sought something closer and more intimate.[38] As a young would-be sculptor in Texas, Janet had discovered a book by Herbert Read in the Dallas public library that had an illustration of Hepworth's *Two Spheres*,[39] 'one of the first pieces of abstract sculpture with which I could identify'.[40] The opportunity to become friends with Hepworth was more than welcome. Following the breakdown of her marriage to Ben Nicholson, Hepworth still felt vulnerable and responded not only to Janet's enthusiasm but also to her background as a sculptor. Then at the peak of her success, Hepworth was receiving important public commissions and exhibitions in London and abroad, often working with one or two assistants.

The two women saw each other most days, spoke frequently on the telephone and developed a bond that was partly anti-men, partly female solidarity and partly a shared sympathy on the plight of being a female artist in a male-dominated society. As someone who had been a sculptor, Janet felt they shared a similar language. 'I formed a deep and lasting friendship with her and learned a great deal about being a professional artist',[41] wrote Janet. Encouraged by Janet, Hepworth found solace in whisky and they often indulged in long drinking sessions. At one point, either recognising or sensing Janet's bisexuality and feeling that people may suspect them of having a lesbian relationship, Hepworth took legal advice and for a time attempted to distance herself from Janet.

Dutifully Janet accompanied Leach on various visits and promotional tours abroad, including one to Scandinavia in October 1960. For this she abandoned her usual trousers, had her dark, wavy hair cropped short, wore a three-quarter-length brown sheepskin coat, flat, low-heeled shoes and borrowed a demure 'little black number' from Barbara Hepworth. Uncharacteristically she added a smear of lipstick. This was followed by a week's holiday in Seville, Spain, which Janet greatly enjoyed, feeling that, being born near Mexico, she had much in common with the Spanish people. Leach, unaccustomed to taking holidays, found it hard to relax and, much to

ABOVE: Janet Leach – Bowl, coiled and thrown, faceted sides, black stoneware, c1980, ⌀ about 30cm

Janet's exasperation, felt that he could only really enjoy himself when he was the centre of attention.

Following Leach's earlier success in the United States, Leach and Janet planned a long promotional tour of the country. This involved Leach lecturing and showing his pots in a series of exhibitions across the length and breadth of the land and was organised in meticulous detail by Janet.[42] As an economy and to facilitate the constant travel, she arranged to hire a car to drive the thousands of miles from venue to venue. In addition she organised clean clothes, motel stops and restocked the exhibitions as pots were sold. It was the first visit to her homeland for eight years and as such presented various emotional challenges, not the least of which was a few days at Threefold Farm. The welcome was warm but having left, promising to return, there were issues to be faced and resolved.

A few days with her parents proved more tense, reflecting the increased distance she felt having made her life elsewhere. Sometime earlier she had observed that, when staying with her parents, there was the 'same conversation, same family disputes and problems – I always feel like I've heard it all so many times before'.[43] Her mother made little secret of her disapproval of her marriage, though Janet felt

ABOVE: Janet Leach – Pot, coiled and thrown in two parts, black stoneware with poured white glaze, 1979, H about 19cm

that, given their difficult relationship in the past, she was unlikely to support any of her choices. With her father, who thankfully got on well with Leach, she played the games she had enjoyed as a child and appreciated establishing a fresh bond with him, but she knew she had little in common with her parents and had no wish to prolong her stay.

Although Janet saw herself as having now left the United States, she still felt a loyalty to her native country, its multicultural tradition and its energy. Having experienced Leach's critical view of Americans expressed several years earlier, she was again dismayed that he made little effort to understand what America or the Americans were about or attempt to see their culture from their point of view. This, by implication, she saw as a further difficulty in their relationship as he either failed or did not bother to understand her ideas or where she had come from.

In many ways the tour was a great success, with appreciative audiences for Leach's talks and buoyant sales of pots, resulting in a profit of £1,000, a handsome sum in 1960. The financial and critical achievement of the visit, Janet hoped, would help cement their marriage as a true partnership, but far from doing so it marked the beginning of a major breakdown in their relationship. Knowing that Leach was planning a trip to Japan the following year she reminded him of her love for the country and spoke of her wish to go with him, funded by the profits of the tour. Such a visit had been discussed, but Leach's friends advised him to go alone.[44] Surprised and alarmed by Janet's suggestion that she accompany him to Japan, far from welcoming her company, Leach's response was to suggest that it might be better if she remained in St Ives to mind the pottery.

For Janet, who regarded Japan as her adopted home and longed to go back to what she saw as 'the well', Leach's reluctance to take her with him affirmed her growing belief that he would not genuinely accept the equality of their relationship. As a result she felt hurt and betrayed by what she saw as his insensitivity and that her role as wife was not accepted seriously by Leach. Janet sought equality within their relationship on her own terms, which included the convention that a wife should, on occasions, accompany her husband. Despite knowing of Janet's love for Japan, her profound admiration

[44] In a letter dated 20. VI. 61 to Lucie Rie, Leach referred to both Rie and Muriel Rose as advising that he should go alone. This letter, which outlines the crisis in their marriage, may or may not have been sent. P.C.

ABOVE: Janet Leach – Bottle with lug handles, coiled and thrown, stoneware, 1979, H about 15 cm

for Hamada and her desire to see him again, Leach's decision failed to acknowledge the depth of her feelings.

Whether Leach felt the need to escape to the country where he was admired and respected unconditionally, thought his friends in the country would not approve of his marriage, or he did want to share his success with his wife is not clear. His decision was a profound disappointment. Psychologically and practically Janet felt that his refusal to recognise fully their marriage as a partnership distanced him from her and as a result allowed her to take a greater measure of freedom.

Bitter and resentful, Janet took Leach's rejection as an indication that their marriage had entered a new phase. Being by nature bisexual, it was around this time that she again started to have love affairs with women, looking for the feeling and affection that she felt was missing from her marriage with Leach. For the first few years of her marriage

ABOVE: Janet Leach – Bowl, thrown and turned, poured glaze decoration, stoneware, 1979, Ø about 20cm

OPPOSITE: Janet Leach, Leach Pottery, c1962 (Photo: Irene Winsby)

to Leach Janet maintained that she had been 'a good wife' and that her liaisons with women only began in earnest following his decision to travel to Japan without her. Inevitably, in a small town, such behaviour was unlikely to go unnoticed. It was typical of a general feeling of antagonism towards Janet by some of Leach's circle of friends that one evening, as he was walking along Fore Street, he was told by one such friend that his wife was having sexual relationships with women.[45] Such news came as a profound shock to Leach who, no matter what problems they were having, had no notion that this was a possibility.

It was a traumatic time for them both with Leach feeling emotionally shattered and utterly bewildered, for although he had long recognised what he saw as the dominant masculine aspects of Janet's nature it had never occurred to him that this would physically involve another woman. In great emotional distress and unsure what to do, he tended to withdraw into silence, preferring to pour out his feelings in letters to his friend Mark Tobey. Janet, while regretting that he had discovered in the way he had, was unapologetic and forthright, arguing that she had the right to seek friendship on her own terms. She later asserted her right to select the relationships she wanted, saying 'I married Bernard because I wanted to. I can sleep with a man, and get bored with a man'.[46]

Feeling completely at a loss as to how to deal with the situation, Leach felt that he must go ahead with his plan to travel to Japan, seeing the country as a welcome reprieve to the intimate and painful problems of his marriage. Slightly to his surprise, in Japan he received chatty, cheerful letters from Janet giving him news of the pottery and the town as if nothing had changed in their relationship. She also told him of her intention to spend three weeks at Threefold Farm at Christmas, much of it, she explained, in the period when the pottery was closed for holidays. When reflecting on their marriage later, Leach concluded that 'consciously or semi-consciously she hoped that in marriage the feminine side of her would emerge and that she wanted leadership from me… by birthright and especially background I tended towards introversion and the feminine… I was just the wrong man for Janet. We were both set. She has become more male and I more female.'[47]

[45] Janet claimed that this was Wilhelmina Barnes-Graham, who later lived in the same black of flats as Leach and was generally highly protective towards him
[46] Conversation with author
[47] Bernard Leach, memoir, December 8, 1963. P.C.

6 A New Beginning
St Ives 1962-74

ABOVE: (L-R) Bernard Leach, Janet Leach, Jeff Oestreich, St Ives, 1975

Janet hoped that, on Leach's return from Japan, they could find a way of living together with each respecting the privacy of the other. But, after a further series of distressing disagreements, she was amazed to discover that Leach, feeling that it would be better if he established his own home separate from her, had privately negotiated the purchase of a flat in a handsome new block being built on Porthmeor Beach, its large picture windows looking towards the Atlantic. Janet only learned of his decision when she found him measuring items of furniture for the new flat. While she had earlier suggested that they should purchase a property adjacent to the pottery to give them more space, it had not occurred to her that Leach would buy and move into a flat of his own. She wanted him to remain, believing that they could work out a way of living together but also fearing that if he moved away from the pottery he would be less inclined to make pots, preferring instead to spend more time pursuing his Bahá'í faith.

Having taken the decision, Leach set about furnishing the flat with pieces from the cottage and started to spend weekends there in 1962, eventually moving in full-time, to be cared for by a succession of housekeepers or a fellow Bahá'í. To this end, Trudi Scott, a Bahá'í who had been present at Janet and Leach's Bahá'í wedding ceremony, hearing of the problems in their marriage, moved to St Ives to be near Leach, even applying for a job in the New Craftsman. Unfortunately for her, Janet had become progressively more antagonistic to Bahá'ís and no job was forthcoming. Much to Janet's disapproval, Scott helped Leach entertain what seemed like a never-ending series of Bahá'í visitors, all of whom, Janet complained, kept him from making pots.

As an investment Janet also acquired a flat in the same block as Leach, occupying it only out of season when it was

ABOVE: Janet Leach – Lidded pot, coiled and thrown, poured glaze decoration, black stoneware, c1980, H about 15cm

not let to tourists, but when she stayed there it did provide a degree of freedom and privacy from the curiosity of workers at the pottery. The new arrangements, of them living separately, while far from ideal, enabled Janet to develop her own circle of friends, in particular to pursue her love affairs, though she was aware that these were constrained by her marriage and the demands on her time as manager of the pottery. When discussing this period in her life, Janet was uncompromisingly straightforward in acknowledging her own commitment to short- rather than long-term affairs. 'If you are a girl you are always going to want to shack up

A New Beginning | 99

ABOVE: Janet Leach – Bottle with lug handles, coiled and thrown, stoneware, c1980, H about 20cm (Photo: Peter Kinnear)

OPPOSITE: Janet Leach – Bottle, coiled and thrown with lug handles, stoneware, 1979, H about 15cm

[1] Janet Leach, interview with author, 1994
[2] Jeff Oestreich (student at the Leach Pottery 1969-71), letter to author, 1997
[3] Janet Leach to Mary Yates and Bill Marshall, letter, 1969. n.d. (Janet Leach Archive, Crafts Study Centre)

and I was not going to as I was married to Bernard… So no relationship could be satisfactory because the girls were always home-hungry, they wanted to shack up'.[1]

Although no longer living together, other aspects of their partnership continued much as before, with Janet continuing to manage the pottery, sort out Leach's exhibitions, organise his diary and help with his arrangements to see friends and entertain students and visitors to supper. Adamant that Leach's true vocation was to be a potter she urged him to spend as much time making pots as possible. To this end most days he drove up to the pottery, where he made and decorated pots and kept in touch with events. A stream of invitations for him to take part in solo or mixed exhibitions meant that a steady output of pots was required and she encouraged him to experiment with dramatic runny ash surfaces as well as intense black-brown temmoku glazes.

With its growing international reputation, the pottery continued to attract a steady stream of students wanting to learn in a working atmosphere. Many brought fresh ideas and suggestions for additional shapes, maintaining a healthy air of enquiry and adventure. In keeping with the growing interest in alternative culture in the 1960s, especially the burgeoning interest in Zen Buddhism – reflected in the influx of 'hippies' into St Ives – the pottery introduced a range of tea bowls, a saki cup and a rice bowl, based on Korean shapes, which for many students were 'most rewarding and difficult'.[2] The latter two forms were introduced by Sigeoshi Ichino, from the Ichino family in Tamba, a potter whom Janet was delighted to welcome, thinking that 'we can show him the value of his inheritance (perhaps by our own inefficiency)… He's a slick, smooth repeat thrower – good guts inside – slightly tough outside – very subtle inside'.[3]

Shortly after arriving in St Ives, Janet was keen to foster a more adventurous response to firing. Aware of the limitations of the three-chamber oil-fired kiln in restricting experiment, in the narrow gap between the large kiln and the side of the kiln shed she built a small kiln, encouraging the students to use this to try out various sorts of firing. At different times salt was introduced into the firing, sawdust

ABOVE: Janet Leach – Bottle, coiled, thrown and beaten, poured glaze decoration, stoneware, 1979, H about 22cm

was blown into the kiln and pots were wrapped in seaweed, all achieving surfaces that bore the effects of the flame. The fact that the kiln was in a confined space, making it difficult to fire, did nothing to deter her; she said that it all added to the excitement. Following problems with the chimney this small kiln was rebuilt in 1962, the new kiln proving slightly more efficient than the first and resulting in innovative pieces that were beneficial to both the pottery showroom and the development of personal ideas. 'Each potter must be allowed and encouraged to "do his own thing",' argued Janet, 'to develop his individual expression in pots alongside his development in throwing standard-ware'.[4]

In the pottery Janet had not only to sort out the day-to-day problems of production but also manage the crew and their different personalities. One of the more challenging was to deal with Horatio Dunn, who, among other duties, was responsible for maintaining the clay supply and packing the pots for dispatch. One of the sons of George Dunn, who, after helping to build the pottery in 1920, had continued to work there, Horatio had a long association with it, but, to Janet's irritation, he ran a series of devious schemes which she saw as an abuse of his position. Dubbed 'the Artful Dodger', his regular series of scams involved the private sale of seconds – pots considered not of first quality – and charging the pottery twice for packing cases. Feeling that such sharp practice had a general demoralising effect and that, far from concealing such deeds, he tended to flaunt them, in a fit of rage she dismissed him, accusing him of 'constant stealing, lying and bad work', and, somewhat ironically, 'heavy drinking'.[5] It was an unpopular decision and many of the crew, led by Leach's grandson John Leach, known as Johnny, who was then working at the pottery, protested that Dunn's many years of loyalty and service should be recognised and he be given the opportunity to change his ways. Unrepentant, Janet insisted that he had had many warnings and that he had become a liability rather than an asset and refused to reverse her decision.

In 1967 Leach, who was now eighty, felt too frail to travel to Japan alone and finally invited Janet to go with him, which she was delighted to accept in what was the first of

[4] Janet Leach, 'Fifty One Years of the Leach Pottery', *Ceramic Review*, no. 14, March/April 1972, pp4-7
[5] Bernard Leach letter to Mark Tobey, January 23, 1963. P.C.
[6] November 1967

ABOVE: Janet Leach – Bowl, coiled and thrown, stoneware, 1959, Ø30cm (Photo: Peter Hoare; Collection: Buckinghamshire County Museum, Aylesbury)

many visits. It was an important change in their relationship, but especially so for Janet, who was returning to the country she loved. How seriously she saw the visit is indicated by the fact that, shortly before she left, she wrote her will, in the event of both her and Leach's deaths. Small bequests were left to the foreman Bill Marshall and to Mary Yates, who was then acting as secretary and shop manager. The remainder of her part of the estate was left to Boots Redgrave, an indication of the depth of her feelings for her. The visit was not only a sign of the enduring nature of her marriage, but, more importantly, a signal of her artistic independence, for she was to have an exhibition in Tokyo, possibly at Hamada's instigation, at the Mitsukoshi Department Store, Tokyo.[6] Although apprehensive, to her surprise and delight, this was hailed critically as a great success and sold out completely. Hamada wrote a brief introduction to her exhibition, setting her pots in context and, much to her satisfaction, concluded that 'her work is good'. During the exhibition Janet felt greatly honoured by a visit from Princess Chichibu, sister-in-law

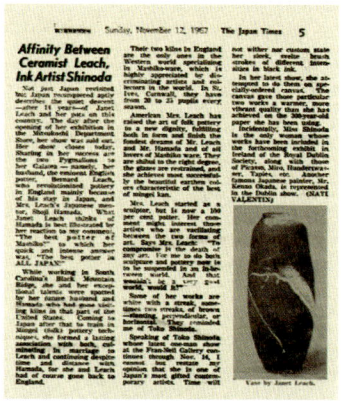

ABOVE TOP: *Japan Times*, November 12, 1967, p5

ABOVE BOTTOM: Janet Leach – Bottle, coiled and thrown, black stoneware, c1980, H about 20cm (Photo: Peter Kinnear)

OPPOSITE: Pages from invitation card for Janet Leach exhibition, Mitsukoshi Department Store, Japan, 1967

[7] Bernard Leach to Mark Tobey, June 9, 1969. P.C.
[8] To coincide with Janet's exhibition, Leach, Hamada and Kanjiro Kawai had a shared exhibition at the Daimaru Department Store in Osaka
[9] October 1967 (Lucie Rie Archive, Crafts Study Centre)
[10] Letter to Mary Redgrave. n.d. (Janet Leach Archive, Crafts Study Centre)
[11] Janet wrote a full account of this visit in 'A Letter from Japan', *Pottery Quarterly*, vol. 9, no. 36, Summer 1970

of the Emperor, who acquired one of her pieces. It was not only royalty that responded positively to her work but, as Leach observed, 'Men (and women) of Tea sit and contemplate her pots for their Western revival, or restatement of glaze textures and qualities. They seem to find a new life in her pots absent in most Japanese pots'.[7] From then on Janet travelled to Japan with Leach not only as his wife, but also as a potter in her own right.[8]

Despite the fact that this was their first visit together to Japan, and involved negotiating ways of being together, the visit was a success. Leach summed up the situation in a letter to Lucie Rie, saying: 'It has not been easy living in tandem but I have done my uttermost to avoid difficulties and we certainly have been able to enjoy many experiences'.[9] What struck Janet most forcibly again was that in the supportive, welcoming atmosphere of his adopted country Leach seemed like a different man. In Japan he was respected and admired, and in response was relaxed and expansive, virtually another person. Having lived with Leach in England, where he seemed overburdened by anxieties and doubts to the point where he appeared to shrink and close up, the change seemed like a miracle, reminding her again of what they had missed by not being able to settle in Japan. As well as helping organise Leach's days and protecting him from what seemed like an endless series of visitors, her broken, often colloquial Japanese was far more effective than his eloquent but old-fashioned *Meiji*, which he had learned fifty years earlier.

With both potters now holding regular exhibitions in Japan, a pattern was established whereby they travelled to the country every two or three years. Struck by the uniqueness of her position as a Western woman exhibiting in Japan, Boots Redgrave suggested that she record her impressions in a daily notebook. Janet, who was an able and amusing writer, was sceptical, reluctant to analyse her feelings, saying 'remember the centipede who couldn't walk when asked which foot to put down first',[10] preferring to absorb and reflect. In March 1969 Janet and Leach returned to attend openings, including a show of her pots at the Osaka Daimoru Department Store,[11] which resulted in discussions about the possibility of holding an annual

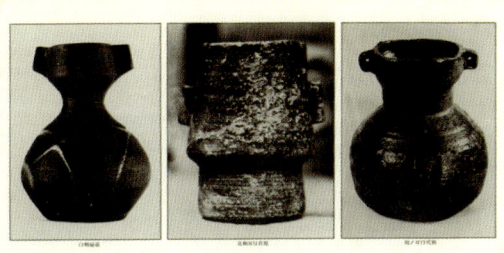
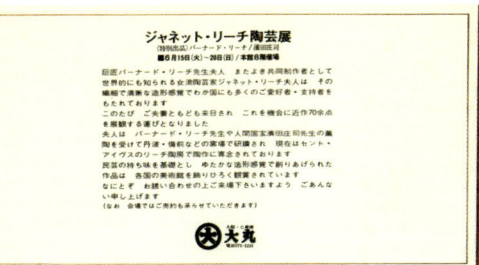
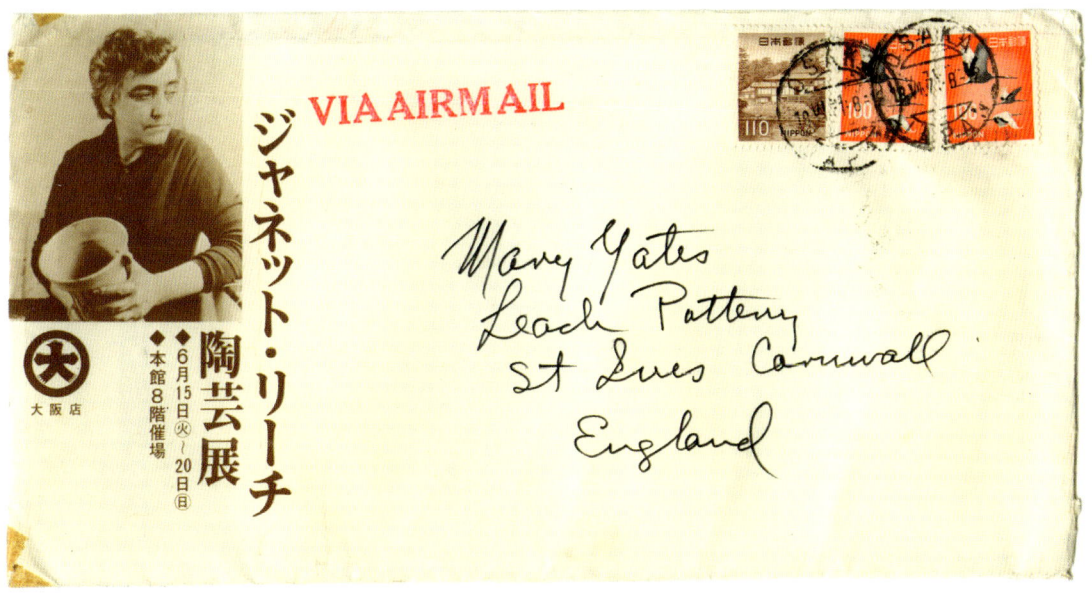

ABOVE TOP: Janet Leach – Bottle, coiled and thrown, stoneware, Tamba, c1970, H about 11cm (Photo: Jason Wason; Collection: Joanna Wason)

ABOVE MIDDLE: Janet Leach – Bottle, coiled and thrown, stoneware, Tamba, c1970, H about 11cm (Photo: Jason Wason; Collection: Joanna Wason)

OPPOSITE: Janet Leach – Bottle, coiled, thrown and beaten, stoneware, 1979, H about 25cm

[12] Janet Leach to Mary Yates and crew, May 6, 1969. (Janet Leach Archive, Crafts Study Centre). Mary Yates worked at the Pottery helping to manage the showroom and acting as secretary
[13] Ibid.

exhibition of her work. Although this did not materialise, her ceramics were acknowledged for their individual qualities, seen to draw on different sources to Leach and resulting in pots that, while responding to traditional Japanese culture, were modern and Western in concept. Visits to Japan also provided opportunities to pursue her independent career by spending time at Bizen and Tamba, where she made pots and investigated traditional kiln firing methods with Kawai's nephew Takeichi.

In Japan Janet was able to escape the routine and administrative demands of the Leach Pottery and enjoy again the ripe, full-bodied stoneware pots made in the old pottery centres of the country. Janet and Leach stayed with the Ichino family in Tamba, where, in the years since she worked there, the market for traditional pots had changed, making the issue of survival for country potteries a real problem. Questions such as to what extent a true tradition of communal craftsmen could be preserved in a meaningful way, or whether this would be replaced by the solitary artist-craftsman as had happened in the West, were endlessly discussed. The '*Mingei* Boom', the rapid rise in commercial interest in handmade craft objects, had also distorted the market, prompting traditional potters to produce self-conscious ware, acquired as art objects rather than for use.

At Tamba, 'using heavy rough mountain clay on a beautiful wheel 300 yrs old',[12] Janet made about eighty pots. She also witnessed a much shorter method of firing the huge kiln whereby it was packed one day, fired the next and opened two days later, a system that knocked several days off the firing. The two weeks were exhilarating; she walked barefoot and ate 'my favourite food' – raw fish and little rice balls, 'Even I drink from the well… I go back into my stockings on 12th to Osaka for exhibition that opens on 14th… The days are numbered so I devour them'.[13] Letters were regularly written to the pottery crew, an indication of Janet's complex feelings towards the pottery that encompassed both affection and resentment. In long, chatty, warm and informal letters, usually addressed to 'Mary Yates and the crew', she described the visits she and Leach made to different potteries and the time spent with Hamada, who was firing a saltglaze kiln. She also asked that they reply with news of the pottery.

ABOVE: Kazue Hamada, Hamada's pottery, Mashiko, 1954

Letters to Boots Redgrave were more personal and passionate, with Janet relating how girdles were not used in Japan because of the floor-based toilets, and marvelling at the care with which Hamada's wife, Kazue, prepared food, on one occasion making a pickled relish using 150 chrysanthemums. She also related how during a stay in a hotel in Cairo she was expected to share a twin-bedded room with a 'most unattractive woman', adding that if 'it had been one of those beautiful Obanarus's... I might have acted differently'.[14] There were often protestations of love, with Janet wanting Boots to be a part of her life 'without losing your independence or personal dignity'. In the letters Janet's loneliness and desire for love and companionship were a recurring theme, the sense of a deep relationship clearly evident, though there seemed to be reluctance on Boots's part to fully reciprocate.

Two years later Janet and Leach were back in Japan when she again made pots – about 120 – at Tamba. There were further exhibitions as well as visits to Tokyo and Okayama, 450 miles south. They were delighted when, on this occasion, Princess Chichibu invited them to her 'lovely new small palace' for an intimate private tea party where 'good English tea' was served in a room filled with pots and drawings. A sensitive and thoughtful patron of the arts, the Princess also made pots. After all the excitement and activity of Japan, Leach returned to St Ives feeling utterly exhausted and immediately collapsed with pleurisy, an illness he had suffered before. Janet, who was recovering from a gall-bladder operation, attempted to nurse him but she was not sufficiently strong and nursing care was taken over by his daughters Eleanor and Jessamine.

By the late 1960s, finding the large, three-chamber kiln at St Ives unwieldy and uneven, Janet built a single chamber kiln, with a 5' x 5' x 5' stacking area, fired by oil, which was often used instead of the large kiln. The three chamber kiln was awkward to pack and time-consuming to fire and, although it held around a thousand pots, it required experienced potters to fire, so disrupting the pottery routine for several days. The smaller kiln was far more convenient and Janet often used it for her experimental firings, packing her small pots inside saggars filled with sawdust and wood

[14] Letter from Janet Leach to Mary Redgrave, 1969-72. n.d. (Janet Leach Archive, Crafts Study Centre)

ABOVE: Janet Leach – Lidded pot, coiled and thrown, incised decoration, stoneware, c1980, H about 17cm

shavings. Despite the high level of loss due to thermal shock, the mottled and textured surfaces achieved the intimate reaction of smoke, flame and fire that she liked.

In addition to making pots and running the pottery, Janet started to become involved in wider aspects of education and craft organisations. She acted as consultant for a new three-year studio pottery course at Cornwall Technical College, Camborne, with Henry Hammond, head of the ceramic department at Farnham School of Art, as external examiner. For Janet it was a new engagement with formal education and she was an enthusiastic and informed supporter.

Both Leach and Janet were committed to international understanding, seeing themselves as ambassadors between

ABOVE: Janet Leach – Bottle with lug handles, coiled and thrown, stoneware, c1980, H about 25cm (Photo: Peter Kinnear)

[15] March 18, 1967 (Leach Archive no. 13881, Crafts Study Centre)
[16] WCC meeting, March 18, 1967. Speakers included Aileen Osborn Webb, President of the WCC, and John Pope-Hennessy, director of the Victoria and Albert Museum (Leach Archive no. 13881, Crafts Study Centre)
[17] Janet Leach 'Poles Apart: World Crafts Council, European Assembly, Cracow, Poland', Crafts, no. 29, November/December 1977, p12
[18] Letter to Victor Margrie, Director of Crafts Council, September 30, 1980 (Janet Leach Archive, Crafts Study Centre)
[19] Janet Leach letter to Richard de la Mare, October 28, 1974 (Leach Archive no. 5329, Crafts Study Centre)

East and West, and were firm supporters of the World Craft Council (WCC), an organisation founded in America by Aileen Osborn Webb and Margaret Patch in 1962. Committed in principle and practice to the international craft movement, both fully supported the WCC's aims and objectives, attending the London conference at the Victoria and Albert Museum in 1967.[15] Henry Rothschild, appointed secretary of the British Section, welcomed their support. The activities of the WCC, thought Leach, were a 'significant moment in the history of the craft' and 'a necessary step in cultural evolution', as the 'young craftsman of any country inherits the cultures of all countries'.[16] Although in full accord with the WCC's aims Janet was not inclined by nature to take official positions within art or craft organisations, but she did commit herself to the organisation as a participant rather than in any official position. 'I am sure the responsibilities of committees and resolutions are very tedious', she wrote to Victor Margrie, then Director of the Crafts Council. Diligently she attended WCC meetings in Poland, Turkey, Ireland and Peru, not as a delegate but because she found them inspiring, commenting that 'the exchange with other craftsmen is as stimulating as the country I was visiting'.[17] Articulate and often critical, she did not approve 'of "how to do it" craft demonstrations… an Eskimo carving a totem pole in Dublin or a flash American potter in Peru demonstrating sophisticated materials to hand model ½" thick walls was unnecessary.'[18]

Although generally physically well for his age and having recovered from pleurisy, Leach's eyesight had begun to cause trouble and, though usually a keen traveller, only reluctantly agreed to go to Japan when the Japan Foundation did him the honour of awarding him the equivalent of the Nobel Prize, worth 5,000,000 yen, roughly £7,127, in 1974. As usual he took on new energy in Japan and although feeling jet-lagged and confused, gave a live television interview at 7.30 in the morning. Janet, shepherding him carefully, sat by his side, describing what was on the table and guiding his hands to handle pots and books. She was amazed at his composure and confidence. Writing later how he 'rose to a magnificent peak and did a magnificent performance, turning to the camera and using

ABOVE: Janet Leach – Dish, coiled and thrown, stoneware, poured glaze decoration, c1980, Ø about 25cm

professional hand movements. I don't know how he did it but he found the reserves out of his love for Japan.'[19]

Shortly after arriving back in St Ives Leach suffered a sudden and dramatic deterioration in his eyesight, glaucoma was diagnosed and an operation performed that saved some peripheral vision. With impaired sight he felt that he could no longer make pots, a decision that Janet was reluctant to accept, believing that he could still see sufficiently well to enable him to do a little decorating. But he was adamant and to all intents and purposes his work as a potter was over. Now eighty-eight and aware of his fragility, he decided to stop smoking despite having smoked heavily for over sixty years. Leach's decision did little to deter Janet's addiction to tobacco.

7 The Accidental and the Incidental
St Ives 1974-79

ABOVE: Janet Leach – Bottle, coiled and thrown, stoneware, c1990, H about 10cm

OPPOSITE: Janet Leach throwing, 1970s

[1] Janet Leach letter to Susan Peterson, September 6, 1978. (Leach Archive no. 5811, Crafts Study Centre)
[2] This was because in the early fifties, Leach divided up his possessions among his four children, David being given the pottery buildings. In return, all had to pay a yearly sum to their father. For a detailed account see Emmanuel Cooper, *Bernard Leach: Life and Work*, Yale University Press, London, 2003
[3] The full story is fascinating. Through a police informant three men – James Love, Guy Tomkins and Michael Shields – were arrested on the Isle of Dogs, and 37 pots and other arts and antiquities recovered. The men were sentenced to terms of imprisonment of 6, 7 and 6 years respectively (Janet Leach Archive, Crafts Study Centre)

With Leach now concentrating on his own writing projects, including a book of poems and one of memoirs, Janet felt that the pottery needed to be organised along more efficient lines. As she pointed out to Susan Peterson, overheads were not reduced just because there were no Bernard Leach pots to sell.[1] Successful exhibitions of her own and Leach's pots in Japan had helped to put the business on a firm financial footing and first it was necessary to resolve the anomaly whereby David Leach still continued to own the pottery buildings on which they were paying rent.[2] A purchase price of £10,000 was finally agreed and the ownership of the property finally passed equally to Janet and Leach.

With the premises now under her control Janet took the opportunity to go ahead with long-planned changes to the property. Pleased, at last, not to have to seek David's agreement, she reorganised production in the light of changing market needs. Visitors coming to pay homage at what she called 'the shrine', to see the collection of Leach pots and tour the pottery, continued to increase and, to give them a more worthwhile experience, a more professional presentation of Leach's pots was needed. A new building was erected that housed a good-sized shop for the sale of standard ware and individual pots, a packing area for dispatching pots, a clay store and a room for displaying the fine collection of Leach's pots that he had given her over the years. The building, a wooden structure sometimes dubbed the 'prefab', seemed perfectly adequate, though when thieves broke in, in 1995, stealing forty-two fine Leach pots, Janet did wonder if a more substantial building was required. The police recovered all but a few of the pots and security was subsequently increased with the installation of an alarm system.[3]

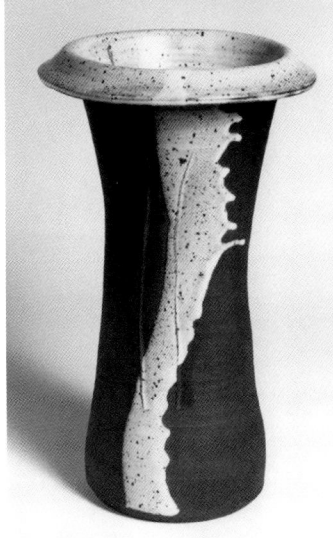

ABOVE TOP: Janet Leach throwing a bowl, c1980

ABOVE BOTTOM: Janet Leach – Bottle, coiled and thrown, poured glaze decoration, black stoneware, 1980, H about 30cm (Photo: Peter Kinnear)

OPPOSITE: Gas kiln ready for unpacking, Leach Pottery, c1980

[4] Janet Leach, letter to John and Donna Reeve, about 1975. n.d. P.C.

To provide Janet with a more private studio, a series of extensive alterations were planned for Pottery Cottage. What had been the old showroom was converted into a studio and the building was altered into two self-contained flats, one upstairs with its own staircase on the side of the building, another on the ground floor for Janet. The studio was fitted with a traditional Japanese wheel set in a box surrounded by shelves with the wheel-head and seat at much the same height to allow Janet to lean over the pot. A Shimpo electric wheel was installed for making some shapes. Following the death of Hans Coper in 1981 she acquired his continental kick wheel, which was fitted with an electric motor to aid throwing; this was set on a platform that again allowed her to lean over rather than sit by the side of the pot as on the English treadle wheel. Like many potters in Japan, Janet preferred to use soft clay for throwing, slurry rather than water to keep the clay lubricated and to use a strip of coarse cloth to throw with, rather than her fingers.

With the market for standard ware shrinking, the original three-chamber oil-fired kiln now seemed too cumbersome for the more modest rate of production, requiring 'too much labour, work and expense for standard ware alone'.[4] In addition it emitted quantities of black smoke, which, as the pottery was now surrounded by housing estates, brought complaints, particularly on Mondays when washing was hung out to dry. Having seen how efficient and relatively straightforward the new gas-fired kilns were and with North Sea Gas now available, so removing the need for a constant supply of cylinders, Janet first considered converting the large kiln from oil to gas but decided that a new, smaller, more efficient gas kiln would be best. This, installed in July 1974, was a great deal more convenient to fire and produced similar results to those from the large kiln. Its smaller size also allowed a more rapid turnaround of pots.

Despite cutting back on the production of standard ware the quality remained variable and stores such as Heal's regularly returned pots they thought not up to the required standard. To help maintain the quality of the standard ware John Bedding, a student apprentice trained at the pottery, returned after working in Japan.

ABOVE TOP: Janet Leach, Bottle, thrown, stoneware, c1990, H about 10cm (Photo: Jason Wason; Collection: Joanna Wason)

ABOVE BOTTOM: Janet Leach – Bottle, thrown, stoneware, c1990, H about 12cm (Photo: Jason Wason; Collection: Joanna Wason)

[5] Janet Leach 'Going To Pot', *Ceramic Review*, no. 71, September/October 1981, p24
[6] Jonathan Sidney, 'Janet Leach – New Pots', *Ceramic Review*, no. 82, July/August 1983, pp30-31
[7] Quoted in Janet Leach 'Going To Pot', *Ceramic Review*, no. 71, September/October 1981, p25

In a new studio and with more time to devote to her own work Janet's pots became looser and more organic in feel. On the veranda outside the studio she had a small kiln installed where she could fire with gas and wood, often burning a fire around the pots, adapting a method based on the firings she had seen at Tamba. This, she said, 'is what I call an exciting creative kiln as compared to placing the pots carefully on a certain shelf… knowing that they will come out exactly right. The firebox commonly used by potters in this country does not bring much fire into contact with the pot.'[5] Using six-inch-long sticks, Janet made the fire around the pots, adding further wood as appropriate to achieve the sintering and marking she admired. Such pieces 'take on all the scars and effects of the firing, bearing the evidence of the bringing together of the clay, fire and wood ash. Drops of dark green glaze mingle with orange and brown flashing and combine with the cratered surfaces to give rich tactile effects.'[6]

Keen to work with natural materials when possible, Janet often quoted the example of Hamada who, when he settled at Mashiko, decided to use the local clay, getting to know its qualities despite the fact that that it was not an easy material to work with. This also fitted in with his desire to keep his tools and glazes as simple as possible. To illustrate how this could be done he often told the story of how, when he was touring America, 'people showed me their very long intricate formulae and they thought I was a peasant because of my glazes [which used local rocks and wood ashes]. What they did not realise was that I was using nature's mixes which are infinitely more complex than we can conceive.'[7]

Rather than buy commercially produced tools and brushes, Janet adopted Hamada's approach, whether by making fine brushes by tying together a tuft of hair clipped from the back of a dog or binding together dry summer grasses with a piece of string for a *hakeme* brush, all of which cost little or nothing. Improvising from materials to hand rather than buying tools, she believed, gave more pleasure and a greater sense of involvement in the decorating process.

The discovery of Ham stone, a naturally occurring yellow-coloured rock from Dorset, was a particularly inspiring find. From this she developed 'an outstanding' glaze with the recipe consisting of Ham stone four parts, white ball

ABOVE: Janet Leach centring clay, c1980

ABOVE LEFT AND RIGHT: Janet Leach throwing a bowl off hump, c1980

ABOVE: Janet Leach – Bowl with lug handles, thrown, stoneware, 1979, H about 10cm

OPPOSITE: Janet Leach exhibition, Japan, c1985

clay four parts and whiting two parts. When fired it produced a trailed glaze that formed rivulets cascading down the surface, rather like a runny ash glaze. To be effective only a thin application was needed. When first applied it behaved more like a slip than a glaze in that it dried extremely slowly; however it could be partly brushed off to produce variations in colour. The thin coating of glaze reacted with the surface to create a 'skin' that seemed to become an integral part of the form, with one critic observing that 'glaze and body fit perfectly – not necessarily in chemical terms, but certainly in aesthetic ones'.[8] This glaze, used on freely faceted or full-bodied shapes, added an element of drama and movement to the surface. When used on different clays, from pale buff to dark red, it picked up any iron oxide from the body, yielding colour variations from yellowish to pale green to black-green, sometimes with orange or reddish glints from underneath.

Although Janet had initially experimented with more formal decoration, this had given way to a more intimate concern with surface quality and texture and their relationship with the overall form. Finger wipe decoration, achieved by pulling the fingers through a layer of glaze before it dried out, was the sort of direct, spontaneous design she favoured, as was beating the surface. Her handling of a fine texture on a globular pot for instance was seen as having 'an overall beaten pattern which made its surface like that of water full of fishes'.[9]

By the early 1970s and with Leach no longer involved Janet felt that having managed the pottery for over twenty years she would like to hand over responsibility for day-to-day production to someone else, giving her more time to spend on her own pots and other activities. Under her management the pottery had become financially profitable so was in a sound state to pass on. Her own health was not good and the extent of her fondness for whisky meant that in the mornings she was somewhat slow to get going, though she usually remained sober until the afternoon. In the event neither of the two appointed managers, both of whom had worked at the pottery and so were familiar with the set up, could either supervise successfully or, more importantly, deal with Janet.

[8] Tony Birks, 'Janet Leach – Recent Pottery', *Ceramic Review*, no. 33, May/June 1975, p16
[9] W A Ismay, 'Pottery by Janet Leach', Southover Gallery, Lewes, February 1981, *Crafts*, no 50, May/June 1981, pp51-52

ABOVE TOP: Janet Leach – Dish, hand-built, incised decoration, stoneware, 1979, L about 18cm

ABOVE BOTTOM: John Reeve

After a long correspondence with Donna Balma, John Reeve's wife, in Vancouver, Janet invited them to return, with Reeve taking over as manager. Although not fully convinced that Reeve would tackle the basic issues of running the crew and maintaining production, Janet embraced the new arrangement with enthusiasm, writing 'there is a gaping hole here that only John could fill… Bill [Marshall] retreats and retreats so that he is carrying no responsibility at all – not even to look in the kiln – or to properly show anyone how to throw a soup bowl'.[10] Confident that any initial teething problems could be resolved she confided to Reeve that she had long seen him as 'Bernard's successor', and then added the final inducement of a promise to amend the will to leave him her half share of the pottery.

Since working as an assistant at the pottery fourteen years earlier Reeve had established a reputation in Canada for his individual pots; despite his professed interest in running the pottery, in his view this did not include making standard ware, a condition Janet found difficult to accept as she saw this as the bedrock of production. As Reeve and Janet attempted to establish a working relationship neither properly listened to what the other expected or required. Janet, while expecting Reeve to provide some of Leach's 'spiritual leadership'[11] within the pottery, basically wanted him to take a hands-on role in managing the workshop and if necessary help to make the larger items of standard ware. In effect she expected him to more or less pick up from where he had left off. Reeve, however, was happy to take over Leach's upstairs studio but with the intention of concentrating on making his own individual pieces; his responsibilities he saw as selecting students and generally overseeing the quality of the ware rather than actually throwing it.

Donna Balma found herself caught in the middle. Encouraged by Janet, she enjoyed the opportunity to make pots under supervision in her studio, pieces which sold well in the showroom, but her loyalties were divided between Janet, who encouraged and helped her, and her husband, who found Janet virtually impossible to work with. The tensions, increasing daily, came to a head when a row broke out when Donna 'arrogantly challenged the legit-

[10] Janet Leach letter to John and Donna Reeve, September 5, 1973. P.C.
[11] Donna Balma letter to author March 25, 1997
[12] Ibid.
[13] The Watergate Trials involved the possible impeachment of Richard Nixon for covering up an illegal bugging attempt made by Republicans at the Watergate headquarters of the Democratic Party during the 1972 elections, eventually resulting in his resignation as President of the United States

ABOVE: Janet Leach – Dish, thrown, stoneware, poured glaze, 1979, Ø about 32cm

imate sincerity of her and BL's marriage',[12] the argument culminating when, in exasperation, Janet hurled a wet pot at her and forbade her to return to the studio. Communication between them finally broke down completely and Reeve felt he had no alternative but to resign his position as manager. The break coincided with the Watergate trials, then making headline news, and led the Reeve family to chant in unison 'Impeach Mrs Leach'.[13]

The mid 1970s were difficult for Janet. She suffered a series of illnesses including shingles, a peptic ulcer and

ABOVE: Janet Leach – Saki set, thrown, stoneware, c1980, H bottle about 12cm

bouts of acute vertigo caused by low blood pressure, on one occasion falling flat on her face with a total loss of balance, putting her out of action for five days. This, together with what many saw as excessive drinking and smoking, caused her, and those around her, much anxiety. The Reeves' departure coincided with the horrific death of Barbara Hepworth in a fire, possibly the result of drinking and smoking in bed. It was a severe loss as Janet not only shared with Hepworth a great empathy as an artist, but they also encouraged each other to take part in activities in the town. At much the same time Bill Marshall announced that, after a forty year-long association with the pottery, he was leaving to set up his own studio. Although he had rarely been in sympathy with Janet or her managerial style, they had maintained a spiky relationship for over twenty years, on her part recognising his invaluable skill and experience. His announcement came while Janet was on an emotionally difficult five-week visit to Texas to see her father who was dying, while attempting to console her mother.[14]

[14] Her father died at De Tar Hospital, Victoria, Texas on May 13, 1976 of arteriosclerotic heart disease and emphysema

Following Bill Marshall's departure a letter written by Leach and Janet, recognising his long and valuable contribution to the pottery, was circulated to many previous employees notifying them of his decision while at the same time suggesting that there might be opportunities for employment as manager. A positive expression of interest came from the American potter Byron Temple. After initially starting work as an apprentice at the Leach Pottery in 1961 he had left to assist Colin Pearson at Aylsford. After setting up his own pottery in the United States he had gained a solid reputation for his range of wood-fired tableware and individual saggar-fired pots with a dark, intense-coloured body. Despite his success in America, Temple was tempted by the idea of change and the opportunity to manage what he regarded as an important pottery workshop. Terms were agreed and he arrived in late August 1978.

The expression of interest by Temple was warmly welcomed by Janet, who, knowing that he was gay, felt that they would have more than pottery in common. She conveniently forgot, or chose not to remember, that, shortly after arriving

ABOVE TOP: Janet Leach – Dish, hand-built, poured glaze, red stoneware, c1980, L42cm (Photo: David Westwood; Collection: Crafts Study Centre)

ABOVE BOTTOM: Byron Temple, c1980

ABOVE: W A Ismay, Janet Leach, c1970s

OPPOSITE: Janet Leach – Bottle, coiled and thrown, stoneware, 1959, H17cm (Photo: Peter Hoare; Collection: Buckinghamshire County Museum, Aylesbury)

as an apprentice, disillusioned by the atmosphere in the pottery and what he saw as lack of leadership, he left, despite the fact that she had secured funding for him from the Gwen Mullins Trust. Having employed and trained potters and produced a well-designed and crafted range of pots in America, Temple appeared to be better able to take over as leader-manager than Reeve, but like his predecessor soon discovered that he and Janet had vastly differing expectations.

Initially there were problems with money. Janet, critical of his low output in the pottery, felt that even the modest monies agreed had not been earned, while he had arrived expecting to work with what he assumed would be a skilled crew. In his view many of the throwers were badly trained and the pots produced were of poor quality, a situation he found difficult to accept. There were also problems with his relationship with Janet. Although he knew of and thought he could handle her fondness for whisky, it was only at close quarters that he saw the scale of the problem. Paradoxically, one of his tasks was to stock up with crates of her favourite brand, bought from a discount supermarket.

ABOVE AND OPPOSITE: Janet Leach exhibition, Japan, c1985

[15] This proposal, in 1975, was to set up a pottery producing a range of standard wares with trainees working alongside experienced potters in premises at Dartington once occupied by Leach. Despite Leach and Janet's lack of interest, the Dartington Training Workshop, advised by David Leach, was set up and a range of tableware produced. It operated as Dartington Pottery until 2006 when it closed and most of the buildings were demolished. The original building used by Leach as a pottery in the 1930s remains
[16] Bernard Leach letter to David Canter and John Lane, September 23, 1975 (Leach Archive no. 5638, Crafts Study Centre)

There was also a bitter confrontation when he challenged Janet over continuing to produce pieces bearing Leach's personal stamp at the pottery. Whether made in moulds or to Leach's exact design, it was not a practice that he felt able to support. His challenge was successful, and production ceased. Not surprisingly, Temple's stay at St Ives was brief, leaving Janet to again take up the reins.

Despite Janet's ambivalent attitude to the standard ware and the difficulties of maintaining quality of production, an offer by the newly formed Dartington Training Workshop to take over production was met with fierce resistance.[15] Leach had had a long and involved relationship with Dartington and so felt a large measure of loyalty to it, for Leonard and Dorothy Elmhurst had been great supporters of his work. They bought his pots and followed his progress; at their invitation he had worked on the Dartington estate in the thirties

with the intention of setting up a pottery; they had financially supported his trips to Japan and funded a major reorganisation of the St Ives pottery by David Leach in the 1930s.

In the 1970s the estate was looking to become more financially viable and had set up the Training Workshop as an educational resource and production workshop. Here it was planned that a regular team of professional potters would produce a range of standard tableware and trainees would learn the skills of making thrown functional wares. While cautiously welcoming the idea of the workshop, both Leach and Janet rejected the idea outright of it producing Leach standard ware, with Leach commenting 'Influence is natural – copying an error'.[16] Janet's opposition was more practical in that she saw it as undermining the pottery's commercial viability. With the pottery often failing to maintain quality the proposal could also be seen as critical of her management.

ABOVE: Janet Leach – Dish, coiled and thrown, poured glaze, black stoneware, c1980, Ø18cm (Photo: David Westwood; Collection: Crafts Study Centre)

[17] Few of the Hamada pots remain at the pottery; they were sold by Janet to secure funds for her 'old age'
[18] Bernard Leach, *Beyond East and West*, Faber and Faber, London, 1978

The Dartington plan also included the setting up of a Leach Museum, a project Janet adamantly opposed, mostly because it would rival the showroom and museum she was in the process of creating at St Ives. The Dartington overtures were turned down flat. Keen to establish her own Leach Museum, which would include a hundred pots by Hamada, Janet applied, unsuccessfully, to the Crafts Council for funding to help set this up as part of the pottery.[17]

As Leach's ninetieth birthday approached, he was deeply involved in writing a book of memoirs, which was published in 1978,[18] though Janet, called on mainly to offer advice, feared it was too long and detailed. Plans for a major retrospective *The Art of Bernard Leach* at the Victoria and Albert Museum, in 1977, however, required much of her attention for she acted as one of the chief co-ordinators, and she saw it as her duty to make this as full and representative as possible. Apart from a relatively modest exhibition *Fifty Years A Potter* in 1961, organised by the Arts

ABOVE: Janet Leach, Bernard Leach, at *The Art of Bernard Leach*, V&A, 1977

Council of Great Britain, no serious critical attention had been devoted to Leach's work in the UK. This was in sharp contrast to Japan where several major retrospectives with handsome catalogues had been held. As a further example of the high regard of the Japanese towards the potter and his pots, the Seibu Department Store in Tokyo planned an exhibition of his individual pieces together with work from the Leach pottery, the first time such a group was to be shown in Japan.

Correspondence between Janet and Carol Hogbin, the organiser of the exhibition at the V&A, reveal the extent to which the project was dogged with indecision, whether wrangling over the costs of putting the show together or the size of the catalogue, with Janet, as Leach's wife and manager of the pottery, regularly striking attitudes and claiming the moral high ground. Initially conceived as a small exhibition, the museum, recognising Leach's significance, expanded it into a major retrospective. Although Janet saw herself,

ABOVE: Janet Leach – Dish, hand-built, stoneware, 1979, L about 15cm

in conjunction with Leach, as prime adviser, she had only been involved from the mid fifties so Leach's son David was also called on. Further ideas on what should be included came from Trudi Scott, who continued to devote much of her time caring for Leach. Understandably, Hogbin sought to include a cross-section from all periods but was occasionally inclined towards what Janet described as 'trivia': unrepresentative pieces such as a coronation mug and a fancy jug that she deemed quirky and unusual rather than good.

While acknowledging the need to be comprehensive, as Janet pointed out, many of Leach's best pots from the twenties were sold in Japan and that in the thirties, having spent little time at the pottery, his output was small, so making chronological coverage difficult. The later, more mature pots, she argued, would make a stronger exhibition. Janet also objected to the inclusion of pieces of inferior quality, giving as an example a small hare plate, which had been sold cheaply as an imperfect 'second'. To Hogbin's amaze-

[19] After all the dithering over the catalogue a lavish illustrated book, also entitled *The Art of Bernard Leach*, edited by Carol Hogbin and based on the exhibition, was published the following year
[20] A form of amyl nitrate
[21] Died May 6, 1979

ABOVE: Janet Leach – Bowl, coiled and thrown, stoneware, c1980, Ø20cm

ment she suggested that, if required, a better one could be made as it was a piece made in a mould. The offer was not taken up. The exhibition eventually included nearly 200 pots plus drawings, prints and working studies.[19] During the opening days of the exhibition Janet was constantly by Leach's side, telling him what was going on, guiding him around and generally acting as protector and mentor. Despite his age, limited sight and the occasional use of a 'popper'[20] to help his breathing, he was well able to cope with the various social events.

Two years later, feeling weak and breathless, Leach was admitted to St Michael's Hospital in Hayle. Although initially agitated by his prolonged stay in hospital he slowly became 'very much at peace and happy during the last ten days', enjoying simple pleasures such as having his hair brushed and the smell of Lilies of the Valley brought in by his daughters. After seeming to be making a recovery he collapsed and died, aged ninety-two.[21]

8 Innovation and Consolidation
St Ives 1979-97

ABOVE: Eileen Lewenstein, Janet Leach, c1985

Reflecting some years later on her busy days immediately after Leach's death, Janet confessed that living and working at the pottery when he was alive and making pots made her feel that she 'was living on the edge of a volcano due partly to Bernard's erratic nature and partly to the nature of St Ives itself where no two days are the same'.[1] Now, with one part of that volcano no longer present, she not only felt a great sense of loss at someone with whom she had had a close if often difficult relationship, but that artistically part of her had changed forever.

Leach had left various instructions following his death. In the early 1970s vast amounts of his archive material – consisting of papers, pots, letters and papers – had been donated to the newly set up Crafts Study Centre, which was then housed at the Holborne of Menstrie Museum, Bath.[2] Following his death his family took over any remaining material other than that at Pottery Cottage. He bequeathed his share of the pottery to Janet, but with no instructions as to its future direction, leaving her to take such decisions as she thought fit. Pottery Cottage was left to her as long as she lived, when it was to revert to his children.

Used to attending to and organising Leach's engagements, the year following his death was an unsettled and difficult time. In spite of their profound disagreements they were bound together by many ties, not least an often grudging admiration for each other's work. Leach had acknowledged Janet's success in organising the pottery and in making it profitable, while she had great belief in him as a potter and admiration for his pots. They also shared a common interest in the pottery, and, perhaps, most importantly, a profound love and respect for Japan. When friends asked if, now that Leach was dead, she would return to the

[1] Janet Leach, 'A Potter's Day', Ceramic Review, no. 146, March/April 1994, p58
[2] Now at University College of the Creative Arts, Farnham
[3] Quoted in Gerry Williams, 'Janet Leach: American Foreigner', The Studio Potter, vol.11, no. 2, June 1983, pp76-93

ABOVE: Janet Leach – Group of pots, coiled and thrown, stoneware, poured decoration, c1985, H tallest about 16cm, (Photo: Peter Kinnear)

States, she was adamant that this possibility held no interest. 'My friends are in England, and with friends you make later in your life you form deeper friendships.'[3] Having established a name as a potter in her own right, not only in Britain but also in Japan, she planned to continue making, devoting as much time to this as possible.

After a period of sorting out and adjustment Janet was now free to run her life and the pottery as she thought best. Almost immediately she brought production of standard ware to a swift end, reasoning that it was something that Leach and David had evolved in the late 1930s and, although she had directed its production for well over twenty years, it was not what she wanted or was really able to continue. From a team of around ten the number of potters was rapidly reduced and within a short time only Trevor Corser, who had trained at the pottery,

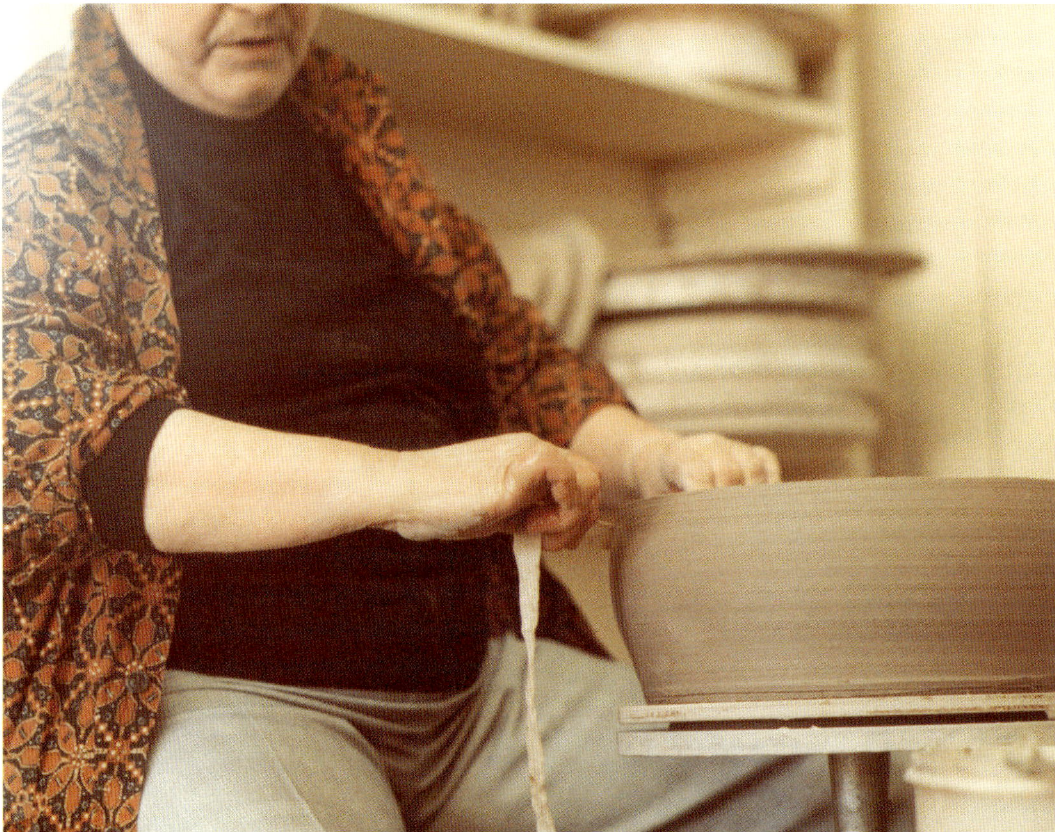

ABOVE: Janet Leach working on base of pot, c1985

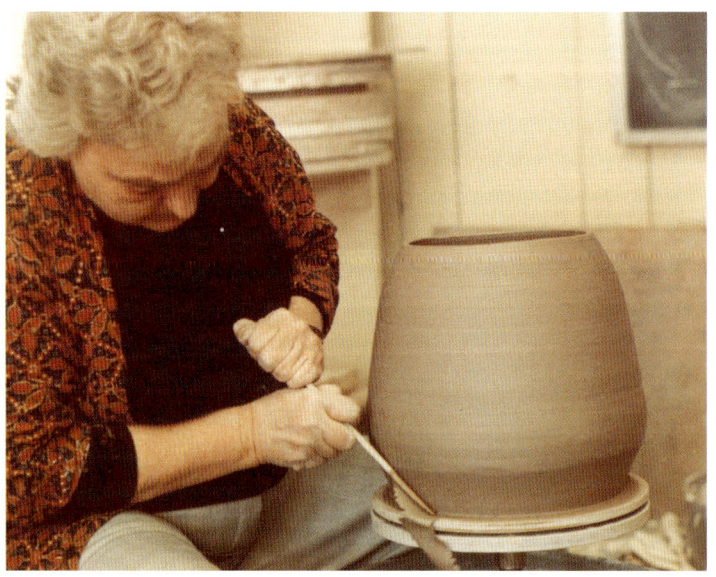

ABOVE LEFT: Janet Leach trimming bottom of pot, c1985   ABOVE RIGHT: Janet Leach working on side of pot with cloth, c1985

ABOVE: Janet Leach incising side of pot, c1985

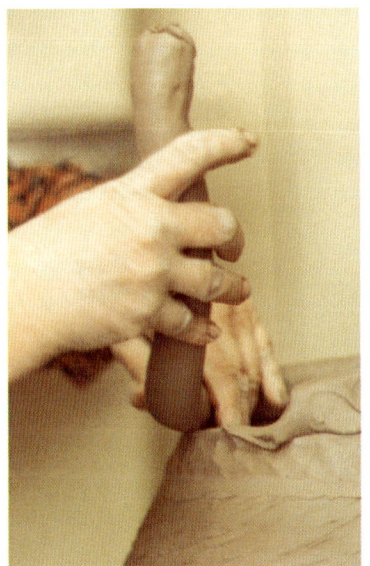

ABOVE LEFT: Janet Leach adding a coil to pot, c1985

ABOVE RIGHT: Janet Leach smoothing and throwing added coils, c1985

Innovation and Consolidation | **135**

ABOVE : Janet Leach – Bowl, thrown with lug handles, stoneware, 1979, H about 6cm

OPPOSITE: Janet Leach, c1987 (Photo: Peter Kinnear)

[4] The BCC had changed its name from the Crafts Centre of Great Britain, and was later to become Contemporary Applied Art in Percy Street, London, where it remains (2006)
[5] W A Ismay 'Pottery by Janet Leach', Southover Gallery, Lewes, February 1981, Crafts, no. 50, May/June 1981, pp51-52

remained making pots, though various assistants were employed, some to run the showroom in the season, to maintain the museum collection and to provide secretarial help. For much of the year they all shared the responsibility of minding the showroom, being 'ready to wash our hands and answer the doorbell at any time', to serve in the shop and even show visitors round the workshop. The period from Christmas to Easter was usually a quiet time for tourists, and Janet saw it as 'a prime working phase' in which she was able to make 'many of my best and "newest" pots'. Together, with occasional help from short-term workers, the two potters made individual pots, with Corser preparing Janet's clay bodies and firing the gas kiln. Part of the workshop premises were let to other craftspeople.

Without Leach to attend to, there was time to become more involved in various activities in St Ives, including assisting at the Penwith Gallery and negotiating with the Crafts Council for funding an applied art showcase within the gallery. For a time she was persuaded to sit on the management committee of what was then the British Crafts Centre[4] in Earlham Street, London, and made regular visits to London with Boots Redgrave to see potters and purchase pots for the New Craftsman. They invariably travelled on the night sleeper from Penzance, booking in to the same room (which they discovered was quiet) in the same hotel, the Coburg (since renamed) on the Bayswater Road. There were also two tours of China with fellow potters arranged by the Craftsmen Potters Association that involved seeing traditional pottery-making centres, which she greatly enjoyed.

Her exhibition at Southover Gallery, two years after the death of Leach was, as one reviewer noted, the first opportunity to see a substantial collection of new pots for three years.[5] This, consisting of 'families' of wares, included ovalled or squared porcelain celadon-glazed vases, some with lively finger-wipe decoration, groups in dark red or black clay, many decorated with poured glaze patterning.

Janet's successful amalgamation of the traditional and modern in her ceramics was succinctly summed up by Tony Birks when he wrote recommending that potters should

have one of her pots 'to remind them that non-alliterative, non-representational potters with traditional backgrounds can pot the pants off more contemporary hot-house ceramics, provided they have the vigour of a Janet Leach'.[6]

Encouraged to continue to show in Japan, Janet was well aware that etiquette demanded a period of mourning before this could happen. An invitation to hold an exhibition there in 1982-3 seemed possible, but she was advised that the pots must look different, reflecting her change of status. Long attracted to the colours and textures of saltglaze stoneware she decided that this would result in pots that were sufficiently different to exhibit. However, knowing that her kiln would not give the rich effects she sought she collaborated with Ian Gregory, a potter in Devon, well-known for his successful salt firings. In the event she took a calculated risk and devoted a whole kiln to her work – her entire exhibition – and although there were mishaps,

ABOVE TOP: Janet Leach – Bowl, thrown and turned, poured glaze, black stoneware, c1980, Ø15cm (Photo: David Westwood; Collection: Crafts Study Centre)

ABOVE BOTTOM: Janet Leach – Bottles with lug handles, thrown, stoneware, c1985, H about 10cm

[6] Tony Birks, 'Janet Leach – Recent Pottery', *Ceramic Review*, no. 33, May/June 1975, p16

ABOVE: Janet Leach – Bottle with lug handles, coiled and thrown, stoneware, c1990, H about 14cm (Photo: Jason Wason)

with shelves collapsing onto the bag wall during the firing, the results were excellent, the surfaces luscious and lustrous, producing the desired mottled and textured surfaces. The pots were shown in Japan to great acclaim.

For the following ten years or so exhibitions were held regularly in Japan, usually in large department stores. These often included up to sixty pots. One entire exhibition was recorded photographically before it was sent. In addition to rounded pots in red clay, black-bodied pots with slashes of white glaze, porcelain pots with a pale celadon often with a pour of black slip, there were a range of slab-built dishes. More unusual were a series of 'bag' or tree-trunk pots, each constructed from a flat slab of clay formed into an upright cylinder from soft clay. The forms billow and move, taking on an inner life that is both sensual and seductive, a feeling enhanced by the textured green-brown-yellow rivulets of the Ham stone glaze.

Innovation and Consolidation | 139

ABOVE: Janet Leach – Bottles, hand-built, black stoneware, c1995, H tallest about 15cm (Photo: Peter Kinnear)

[7] See Joanna Wason, 'Janet Leach', *Ceramic Review*, no. 221, September/October 2006, pp42-5
[8] 'Janet Leach – New Pots', Contemporary Ceramics, London, November 1995
[9] Janet Leach, 'A Potter's Day', *Ceramic Review*, no. 146, March/April 1994. p58
[10] The death certificate listed bronchopneumonia and cerebrovascular disease

With St Ives set to expand dramatically with the opening of the Tate Gallery, dedicated to artists associated with the town and planned for the early 1990s, Janet saw fresh opportunities for promoting the showroom and Leach Museum. With a view to representing the work of Bernard Leach in Tate St Ives, the director Mike Tooby approached Janet with the idea of borrowing pots from her collection, but he either got the timing or the tone wrong, for Janet refused point-blank. Subsequently she had little involvement in the Tate, although it regularly had a showcase of Leach's pots on loan from the Wingfield Digby collection and often placed pots by other potters in other corners of the gallery.

Throughout the nineties Janet continued to make pots, often with the help of an assistant. These included Joanna Wason, wife of Jason Wason who had worked at the pottery in the 1970s, who helped by making smaller pieces.[7] Making pots became more difficult as her health declined,

ABOVE: Janet Leach – Bottles, hand-built, black stoneware, c1994, H about 20cm (Photo: Jason Wason)

though in 1996 the pottery had a turnover of over £42,000. The drinking and smoking took its toll, she put on weight and suffered falls through low blood pressure, often sustaining physical injury. Nevertheless, she held an exhibition in 1995,[8] and one at Austin Desmond Fine Art, London, in 1997, which would be her last. Around this time she wrote 'Many potters retire but I still feel that my function in life is to make pots. I do not knit or garden. It is my hope to continue making pots and good pots',[9] an intention she had followed for much of her life.

In the latter few months, more or less confined to bed and cared for by friends, she attempted to sort out her affairs but was aware of her increasingly frail condition. She died on September 12, 1997.[10] Her funeral, at Penmount Crematorium, Truro, five days later, as she requested, involved no ceremony nor eulogy, but a small group of silent mourners attended to pay their own respects. No one tied a yellow ribbon.

Postscript

ABOVE: Janet Leach – pots in the showroom, 1992

Following Janet's death in 1997 the chief legatee was Mary (Boots) Redgrave, the friend with whom she had opened the New Craftsman in St Ives. Pottery Cottage returned to the Leach family and was put on the market. This sale was complicated by questions of access, as no legally established right of way had been recognised across land belonging to the pottery. Mary Redgrave inherited virtually all Janet's estate, including the business, the pottery buildings and contents, the Leach and Hamada pots, all Janet's possessions and Janet's share of the New Craftsman. Shortly after, books, certain pots and other artifacts from the estate came up for auction at Bonhams, South Kensington in 1998, and although attempts were made to save part if not all the collection for the nation or to keep it together in some way, this was unsuccessful and it was sold in various lots, though some books were acquired by the School of Oriental and African Studies, London, and the Sainsbury Centre for Visual Arts.

Boots Redgrave continued to maintain the pottery and showroom as a viable concern, with the workshop occupied by Trevor Corser and Joanna Wason. The museum collection remained open to the public. The showroom was stocked with pots from the two resident potters, supplemented by pieces from potters who had previously worked at, or been associated with, the pottery. A steady stream of visitors came, many from abroad, and though many wanted to see the kiln shed and workshops, these were in a poor state of repair and it was not practical to allow the public access. The kiln shed, built in 1920 by traditional methods, threatened to collapse and further damage the three-chamber kiln, which, though not in use, was still largely intact. Recognising the importance of the Leach Pottery as a vital

ABOVE: Janet Leach standing in the doorway of the Leach Pottery Showroom, 1992

part of Britain's cultural heritage, the external building structure was given class B protection as a listed property, at least preventing it from being demolished. In 1999 Alan Gillam, a local hotelier, bought the pottery and Pottery Cottage and in the process of restoring the cottage revealed a large and handsome fireplace lined with tiles decorated by Leach. The ground floor of the cottage was converted into a new exhibition space and Leach Museum that included choice pieces by previous students at the pottery. Trevor Corser and Joanna Wason continued to work at the pottery until 2005 when the premises were acquired by Penwith District Council as part of establishing the Bernard Leach Pottery Trust, which will take over the property and preserve it as a living museum and educational centre.

Selected Exhibitions

Janet Leach and Richard Hieb
Osaka Takumi Trading Co, Japan, June – July 1955

Janet Leach and William Marshall
Primavera, London, October 14-24, 1959

Janet Leach – Pots
Primavera, London, June 1965

Janet Leach – Pots
Mitsukoshi Department Store, Tokyo, Japan, November 1967

Janet Leach and Lucie Rie – Pots
Primavera, London, 1968

Janet Leach – Pots
Osaka Daimoru department store, Japan, March 1969

Janet Leach – Pots
Japan, 1972

Janet Leach – Recent Pots
British Crafts Centre, London, March 1973

Janet Leach – Pots
Amalgam, London, May 1975

Janet Leach – Recent Pots
British Crafts Centre, London, March 1976

The Leach Pottery
Amalgam Gallery, London, March – April 1977

Janet Leach – Recent Ceramics (with David Burnham)
Burleighfield International Arts Centre, High Wycombe, March 1978

Janet Leach – Pottery
Southover Gallery, Lewes, February 1981

Janet Leach – Pots
Japan, 1982

Janet Leach – New Pots
Craftsmen Potters Shop, London, April 1984

Janet Leach – Pots
Japan, 1985

Japonisme – Japanese Reflections on Western Art
Northern Centre for Contemporary Art, Sunderland, September – November 1986

Ruth Duckworth and Janet Leach – New Ceramics
British Crafts Centre, London, October – November 1986

Janet Leach – New Pots
Contemporary Ceramics, London, November 14-25, 1989

Janet Leach – Pots
Ceramic Series, Aberystwyth Arts Centre, November 1990

Janet Leach – New Pots
Contemporary Ceramics, London, November – December 1995

Janet Leach – Pots
Austin Desmond Fine Art, London, January 1997

Chronology

1918   Born Nell Janet Darnell, March 15, 1918, Grand Saline, Texas, USA

c1932   Attends art classes

c1934   Works as sculptor's assistant making a diorama on the history of Texas

1937   Travels to New York by Greyhound bus. Enrols at small art school where sculpture is taught by Robert Cronbach. Works as sculptural assistant as part of New Deal with Robert Cronbach

c1940   Marries Joe Turino, shipyard worker

1941   Outbreak of war, works in port of embarkation

1942   Works as welder for Bethlehem Steel in shipyard; obtains a full welder's licence

1946   Assists Robert Cronbach. Works with disadvantaged children

1947   Works as sculptor, mostly in metal

1947   Studies at Inwood Pottery. Reads Bernard Leach's *A Potter's Book*

1948   Sets up pottery teaching studio in Rockland State Mental Hospital, New York State

1949   Settles at Threefold Farm, sets up pottery studio

1950	Attends lecture by Bernard Leach in New York
1950-1	Attends Summer school at Alfred University
1952	Attends two-week conference at Black Mountain College
1954	Moves to Japan to work with Hamada at Mashiko. Meets Leach again; they form a close relationship
1954	Moves to Tamba to work in Ichino traditional workshop, December
1955	First exhibition in Japan, shared with Richard Hieb, June
1956	Moves to St Ives, England, marries Bernard Leach, Penzance Registry Office, March 26
1960	Tours Scandinavia with Leach
1960	Tours United States with Leach, who lectures and exhibits pots, visits Threefold Farm and parents
1962-3	Bernard Leach moves to own flat in St Ives, leaving Janet to manage Leach Pottery
1967	Janet and Bernard Leach visit Japan, the first of many visits
1972	Pottery buildings bought from David Leach, a series of changes instigated
1974	Bernard Leach stops potting
1979	Bernard Leach dies; Janet becomes sole owner of the Leach Pottery
1997	Dies September 12, 1997 of bronchopneumonia and cerebrovascular disease, St Ives. Interred Penmount Crematorium, Truro, Cornwall, September 17

Bibliography

Yoshiko Uchida, 'To Learn Local Methods', *Nippon Times*, n.d. (c. July 1954)

Janet Darnell, 'Impressions of Life in Rural Japan', 1955. P.C.

Janet Leach, 'With Hamada in Mashiko', *Pottery Quarterly*, vol. 3, no. 11, Autumn 1956

Janet Leach, 'Tamba', *Pottery Quarterly*, vol. 4, no. 13, Spring 1957

Michael Casson, *Pottery in Britain Today*, Tiranti, London, 1967

Tony Birks, *Art of the Modern Potter*, Country Life, London, 1967

J P Hodin 'Janet Darnell Leach', *Pottery Quarterly*, vol. 9, no. 33, Autumn 1967

Janet Leach, 'A Letter from Japan', *Pottery Quarterly*, vol. 9, no. 36, Summer 1970

Muriel Rose, *Artist Potters in England*, Faber and Faber, London, 1970

Janet Leach, 'Fifty One Years of the Leach Pottery', *Ceramic Review*, no. 14, March/April 1972

Eileen Lewenstein, 'Janet Leach', *Crafts*, no. 15, July/August 1975

Tony Birks, 'Janet Leach – Recent Pottery', *Ceramic Review*, no. 33, May/June 1975

'Janet Leach – Recent Pots', *Ceramic Review*, no. 39, May/June 1976

Ian Auld, 'The Leach Pottery 1977', March 11 – April 12, Amalgam Gallery, London, *Crafts*, no. 26, May/June 1977

Janet Leach, 'Cornwall Technical College: Ceramics', *Crafts*, no. 28, September/October 1977

Janet Leach, 'Poles Apart: World Crafts Council, European Assembly, Cracow, Poland', *Crafts*, no. 29, November/December 1977

William Edwards, 'Recent Ceramics by Janet Leach and Ceramic Sculpture by David Burham', *Crafts*, no. 32, May/June 1978

W A Ismay, 'Pottery by Janet Leach', Southover Gallery, Lewes, February 1981, *Crafts*, no. 50, May/June, 1981

Janet Leach, 'Going To Pot', *Ceramic Review*, no. 71, September/October 1981

Gerry Williams, 'Janet Leach: American Foreigner', *The Studio Potter*, vol. 11, no. 2, June 1983

Jonathan Sidney, 'Janet Leach – New Pots', *Ceramic Review*, no. 82, July/August 1983

Tony Birks, 'Janet Leach', *Crafts*, no. 63, July/August 1983

Janet Leach, 'Shoji Hamada', *Ceramic Review*, no. 101, September/October 1986

John Houston, 'Ruth Duckworth and Janet Leach – New Ceramics', *Ceramic Review*, no. 102, November/December 1986

Emmanuel Cooper, 'Janet Leach – Sculptural Potter', *Ceramic Review*, no. 120, November/December 1989

Emmanuel Cooper, 'Janet Leach', Ceramic Series, Aberystwyth Arts Centre, leaflet no. 44, November 1990

Janet Leach, 'A Potter's Day', *Ceramic Review*, no. 146, March/April 1994

'Janet Leach – New Pots', *Ceramic Review*, no. 156, November/December 1995

Marion Whybrow, *The Leach Legacy: St Ives Pottery and its Influence*, Sansom & Co, Bristol, 1996

Moira Vincentelli, *Women and Ceramics: Gendered Vessels*, Manchester University Press, Manchester, 2000

Emmanuel Cooper, *Bernard Leach: Life and Work*, Yale University Press, London, 2003

Joanna Wason, 'Janet Leach', *Ceramic Review*, no. 221, September/October 2006

Footnotes

P.C. refers to Private Collection
n.d. no date

Collections

Work is included in many British collections, including Buckingham County Museum, Aylesbury; Crafts Study Centre, Farnham; Fitzwilliam Museum, Cambridge; Shipley Art Gallery, Gateshead; Victoria and Albert Museum, London; Manchester Art Gallery; Tate St Ives; Potteries Museum, Stoke-on-Trent. International collections include Museum Boyman-Van Beuningen, Rotterdam, the Netherlands, and Newark Museum of Art, New Jersey, USA.

Illustrations

Captions indicate pieces in private and public collections. Every effort has been made to contact copyright holders and to credit owners and photographers. Many apologies for credits not given.

Acknowledgments

Many people have helped in the preparation of this book, whether with conversations about Janet Leach, the loan of papers and photographs, interviews and reminiscences.
I would like, in particular, to mention Rob Airey (Cornwall County Council), the American Potters Association, Mary Barringer, John Bedding, Sally Burns at Threefold Farm, Trevor Corser, Professor Simon Olding and Jean Vacher at the Crafts Study Centre, Ben Eldridge, Susan Daniel McElroy at Tate St Ives, Ian Gregory, David Horbury, Michael Hunt at the New Craftsman, Helen Joseph at Shipley Art Gallery, Gwyn Hanssen Pigott, Phil Rogers, Henry Rothschild, Pauline Rothschild, Linda Sandino, Paul Vibert, Jason Wason, Joanna Wason, Gerry Williams and Irene Winsby. My thanks to them all.

Index

BL – Bernard Leach;
JL – Janet Leach;
n – footnote

Albers, Josef 24*n*
Alfred University 27
anthroposophy 10, 26 and *n*, 34
Art of Bernard Leach, The (exhibition) 128-131
Arts Council of Great Britain 88, 128
Auld, Ian *The Leach Pottery 1977* 84*n*
Austin Desmond Fine Art (London) 141
Bacon, Francis 90 and *n*
Bahá'í 45, 46, 62, 88, 98
Balma, Donna 74, 76*n*, 114*n*, 120 and *n*, 121, 122
Barlow, Sir Alan and Lady 76*n*
Barnes-Graham, Wilhelmina 90, 96*n*
Batterham, Richard 68, 72 and *n*
Bauhaus 28, 30
Bedding, John 114
Bernard Leach Pottery Trust 143
Bertha Shaefer Gallery (New York) 18*n*
Binney, Joe 68
Binns Medal 27
Birks, Tony 136 and *n*; *Janet Leach – Recent Pottery* 118*n*, 136*n*
Bizen 5, 8, 11, 12, 57, 106
Black Mountain College 24*n*, 28, 30 and *n*, 32, 34
Bonhams 142
Bonovitz, Jill 78 and *n*
Boswells 76*n*
British Crafts Centre (later Contemporary Applied Arts) 136 and *n*
British Museum 76*n*
Brough, Alan 74
Bunraku puppets 42
Canfield, Miss 28*n*
Cardew, Michael 6 and *n*, 76 and *n*
Castle, Len 74
Chambers, Mrs 50
Chichibu, Princess 103, 108
Chinese ceramics 5
clay bodies 8, 52, 66, 70, 80, 114, 116, 136
Contemporary Applied Arts 136*n*
Contemporary Ceramics 140*n*
Cooper, Emmanuel *Bernard Leach: Life and Work* 4*n*, 112*n*; *David Leach* 4*n*

Coper, Hans 114
Corser, Trevor 133, 136, 142, 143
Courtney, Ralph 26, 28n
Craft Centre of Great Britain 84n
Crafts Council 86, 110 and n, 128, 136
Craftsmen Potters Association 136
Crafts Review 76n
Crafts Study Centre (Farnham) 4, 66n, 132 and n
Cronbach, Robert 18 and n, 24
Culot, Pierre 74
Dailey, Mary 27
Daimaru Department Store 104 and n
Darnell, Charles Walter (father of JL) 14, 62n, 122
Darnell, Ollie Rebecca (mother of JL) 14, 93, 122
Dartington Training Workshop 126 and n, 127-128
da Silva, Helena 74
de la Mare, Richard 110n
de Waal, Edmund *The event of a thread, the event of clay: Black Mountain College and the Crafts* 30n
Dobble, Joe 70
Dormer, Peter *The New Ceramics: Trends + Traditions* 22n, 78n
Dunn, Dinah 68, 72 and n
Dunn, George 102
Dunn, Horatio 68, 102
Elmhurst, Dorothy 126
Elmhurst, Leonard 126
Emms, Derek 74
Farnham School of Art 109
Federal Arts Projects (FAP) 5, 18 and n, 20
Fieldhouse, Murray 76 and n
Fifty Years A Potter (exhibition) 128-129
First Nation ceramics 6, 11, 33-34
Ford, Tony 86 and n
Fosdick, Marion 27
Gillam, Alan 143
glazes 8, 12, 33, 74, 79, 82, 116, 118 and n, 136, 138-139
Goetheanum 10
Goulet, Lorrie 24 and n
Green Meadow School, 27
Gregory, Ian 8, 138
Grotell, Maija 24 and n
Gwen Mullins Trust 124
Hakone Museum 42
Hamada, Atsuya 74
Hamada, Kazue 108
Hamada, Shoji 10, 11, 28, 30 and n, 32 and n, 33, 34, 36 and n, 40 and n, 42 and n, 44, 46, 47, 48, 50, 58, 59, 60, 62, 74, 78, 82, 95, 103, 104n, 106, 116, 128 and n, 142
Hammond, Henry 109
Hanssen, Louis 74n

Hanssen Pigott, Gwyn 70
Harder, Charles M 27
Harrison, Martin *In Camera* 90*n*
Heal's 84*n*, 114
Henry, Michael 74
Hepworth, Barbara 72*n*, 85, 88, 91, 92 and *n*, 122
Heron, Patrick 90
Hieb, Richard 34, 35, 44, 56, 57, 58
Hilton, Roger 90
Hodin, JP *Janet Darnell Leach* 10*n*, 12*n*, 78*n*
Hogbin, Carol 129, 130; *The Art of Bernard Leach* 130*n*
Horne, Frances 62 and *n*
Horne, Margery 62
Hudson Walker Gallery (New York) 18*n*
Ichino family 47, 48, 51, 100, 106
Ichino, Hirouki 48
Ichino Pottery 47, 48
Ichino, Sigeoshi, 100
Ichino, Toshio 48, 52
Inwood Pottery Studios 24 and *n*, 25
Isaacs, Harry 74
Ismay, WA 82 and *n*; *Pottery by Janet Leach* 10*n*, 82*n*, 118*n*, 136*n*
Japan Foundation 110
Japanese ceramics 6, 10 and *n*, 11-12, 30, 38, 39, 106
Japanese Folk Craft Museum 38
Jenkins, Richard 70
Jenyns, Soame *Japanese Pottery* 10*n*, 12*n*
John, Gwyn (later Gwyn Hanssen Pigott) 70, 74 and *n*
Jones, Billie (aunt of JL) 16
Kawai, Kanjiro 44 and *n*, 104*n*, 106
Kawai, Takeichi 106
Kenny, John 27
Kenzan 44
kilns, gas-fired 27, 114, 116, 136; Korean-type 48, oil-fired 66, 100, 108, 114 and *n*; snake 52, 54; three-chambered 66, 100, 108, 114, 142; wood-fired 8, 27, 52-53, 116
kishiku 11
Kjaersgaard, Anna 74
Korean ceramics 5, 12
Lanyon, Peter 90
Leach Archives 4, 30*n*, 47, 66*n*
Leach, Bernard 4, 5, 10, 12, 24*n*, 25, 27, 28, 30 and *n*, 32, 33, 34 and *n*, 35, 36, 38, 39, 42, 44 and *n*, 56, 57, 58 and *n*, 60, 61, 62, 64, 66, 68, 70, 74 and *n*, 76, 78, 79, 80, 82, 84 and *n*, 85, 86-88; 90, 91, 92 and *n*, 93, 94 and *n*, 95, 96 and *n*, 98, 100, 102 and *n*, 103, 104 and *n*, 106, 108, 109, 110, 111 and *n*, 112, 118, 120, 123, 126, 127, 128, 129, 130-131, 132, 133, 136, 140, 142, 143; *The American Journey with Yanagi and Hamada* 30*n*; *Beyond East and West* 34*n*, 84*n*, 128 and *n*; *A Potter in Japan* 44*n*; *A Potter's Book* 24*n*, 25, 27, 28

Leach, David 4, 45, 58, 60-61 and *n*, 64, 68, 90*n*, 91, 112, 126*n*, 127, 130, 133

Leach, Janet Darnell (née Nell Janet Darnell)

LIFE: birth 5, 14; childhood 14, 16; education 14, 16, 18; her relationship with her parents 14, 93-94; assists Spanish refugees fleeing to Mexico 16; lives in New York 17, 18, 20, 22, 24-25; studies with Robert Cronbach 18 and *n*, 24; marries Joe Turino 20; assists with war effort 20, 22; trains as welder 22 and *n*; works at Inwood Pottery Studios 24 and *n*, 25; lives at Threefold Farm 25, 26-28, 34, 36; partnership with Mary Dailey 27; attends BL lectures in New York 27, and at Black Mountain College 28, 30; sees Hamada at work at the wheel 32 and *n*; relationship with BL 34, 38, 44-46, 57-58, 60, 61, 62 and *n*, 64, 76, 79, 84-85, 86-88, 93, 94-96, 98, 103, 104 and *n*, 120-121 and *n*, 132; moves to Japan 36, 38; stays with Hamada 39-40 and *n*, 42, 44, 46; moves to Tamba 46*n*, 47-48 and *n*, 50-52, 54-56; moves to St Ives 61, 62; marriage to BL 62 and *n*; health 74-75 and *n*; 108, 111, 118, 121-122, 140, 141; heavy smoking 74, 76, 111, 122, 141; fondness for alcohol 74, 76, 92, 102, 118, 122, 124, 141; friendship with Mary 'Boots' Redgrave 90, 91 and *n*, 92, 103, 104, 108 and *n*; acquires Anchor House 91; friendship with Barbara Hepworth 91, 92 and *n*; travels to Europe 92; visits US 93-94, breakdown in relationship with BL 94-95; starts sexual relationships with women 95, 96 and *n*; lives apart from BL 98; buys flat at Porthmeor Beach 98; travels to Japan with BL 102-103, 108, 110-111; with BL acquires pottery buildings from David Leach and erects new building 112 and *n*; alterations made at Pottery Cottage 114; installs gas kiln at Leach Pottery 114; appoints John Reeve as manager of Leach Pottery 120; her father dies 122*n*, appoints Byron Temple as manager of Leach Pottery 123; involvement in *The Art of Bernard Leach* exhibition 128-131; death of BL 131; death of JL 141, 142;

CAREER: critical responses to her work 4, 5, 12, 42, 57, 82 and *n*, 84 and *n*, 103, 104, 106, 118, 136 and *n*, 138, 139; in shadow of BL 4, 66 and *n*, 78, 84, 85, 86; as sculptor 5, 6, 8, 20 and *n*, 22, 24; builds experimental kilns 8, 27, 100, 102; works as sculptural assistant 16; works at Inwood Pottery Studios 24-25; teaches at Rockland State Mental Hospital 25, 68; gives pottery classes 27; works in Tamba 46*n*, 47-48 and *n*, 50-52, 54-56; works at Bizen 57; management of the Leach Pottery 64, 66, 68-70, 72, 74, 78, 86, 94, 98, 100, 102, 112, 114, 118, 120, 122, 123-124, 126 and *n*, 127; exhibits at Primavera 84; chooses to work under Leach name 84-86, opens New Craftsman Gallery 91; exhibits at Mitsukoshi Department Store 103, and Osaka Daimoru Department Store 104; acts as consultant to Cornwall Technical College 109, exhibits in Japan (1980s) 138-139; final exhibitions at Contemporary Ceramics and Austin Desmond Fine Art 141;

PERSONALITY AND BELIEFS: physical appearance 4, 34, 92; motivation for her marriage to BL 4, 58, 60, 85, 86; personality of 4, 5, 12, 58, 62, 64, 72, 86, 88, 120, 122, 129; influences on her work 5, 6, 12, 78, 79, 84; pride in Texan origins 6, 14; preferred shapes and techniques 6, 8, 52, 54, 74, 78, 79, 80, 82, 83-84, 100, 102, 114, 116 and *n*, 118 and *n*, 138; her pots as a reflection of her character 8, 12; masculine attributes 8, 96; her pottery stamp 8-9; sexuality 9, 58, 86, 92, 95, 96, 98, 99-100 and *n*, 123; her philosophy of pottery 10-11, 25 and *n*, 28, 34, 56-57, 78 and *n*, 102; political views 16, 18, 20, 25; her view of other potters' work 34, 48, 68, 84; attitude to Bahá'í faith 46, 62, 88, 98; opinion of BL's pots 78 and *n*, 82, 132; loyalty to American values 94; love of Japan 94, 103, 132; support for World Craft Council 110 and *n*;

WRITINGS: *Fifty One Years of the Leach Pottery* 68*n*, 80*n*, 102*n*; *Going to Pot* 116*n*; *Impressions of Life in Rural Japan* 56*n*; *Japanese Diary* 40*n*; *A Letter from Japan* 104*n*, 108*n*; *My First Three Weeks in Japan* 42*n*; *Poles Apart: World Crafts Council European Assembly* 110*n*; *A Potter's Day* 78*n*, 132*n*; *Shoji Hamada* 10*n*, 28*n*, 32*n*; *Tamba* 46*n*; *Untitled Document CSC* 92*n*, *Why I Came to Study in Japan* 56 and *n*; *With Hamada in Mashiko* 32*n*, 38*n*, 40*n*

Leach, Jessamine 108
Leach, John 102
Leach, Laurie 64
Leach, Maurice 64
Leach Museum 66, 128, 140, 142, 143
Leach Pottery (St Ives) 4, 5, 45, 58, 60, 62, 64, 66 and *n*, 68-70, 72, 74 and *n*, 76, 84 and *n*, 86, 90, 94, 96, 100, 102, 106 and *n*, 108, 109, 112 and *n*, 114, 118, 120, 121, 122, 123, 124, 126-127, 132, 133, 136, 140, 141, 142, 143
Lebovitch, Donatienne 38
Lewis, Glenn 74
Liberty (London department store) 84*n*
Livingstons, The (friends of BL) 38
London University, School of African and Oriental Studies 142
Love, James 112*n*
Lowerdown Pottery (Bovey Tracey) 60*n*
Manchester City Art Gallery 84*n*
Margrie, Victor 110 and *n*
Marshall, Scott 68
Marshall, William (Bill) 68, 84, 100*n*, 103, 120 and *n*, 122, 123
mattcha (tea ceremony) 44 and *n*
McMeekin, Ivan 70
Meiji 104
Milne, John 91
Mingei 28 and *n*, 48, 106
Mingeikan (Japanese Folk Craft Museum) 38
Mitsukoshi Department store (Tokyo) 103
Molochite 82 and *n*
Mud and Water Man (film about Michael Cardew) 6*n*
Museum of Modern Art (New York) 92*n*

Nagoro, Minnie 27
Nance, Dicon 76
Nance, Eleanor 62, 76, 108
Nance, Robert 90*n*, 91
National Academy of Design (New York) 24
New Craftsman Gallery (St Ives) 91, 98, 136, 142
Newland, Bill 78
Nicholson, Ben 88, 92
Oestreich, Jeff 100*n*
Okuda, Mr 48
Osaka Takumi Trading Co 57
Pandit, Nurmala 74
Parker, Miss 38*n*
Patch, Margaret 110
Pearson, Colin 123
Pendley Manor 76 and *n*
Penwith District Council 143
Penwith Gallery (St Ives) 88, 90, 136
Perkins, Dorothy, 27
Perkins, Lyle 27
Peterson, Susan 27, 34 and *n*, 112 and *n*; *Bernard Leach: Two Recollections* 30*n*
Play School Association 24
Pollock, Jackson 8
Pope-Hennessy, John 110*n*
Pottery Quarterly 76*n*
Primavera 84
Quick, Kenneth 72 and *n*
Read, Herbert 92
Redgrave, Mary ('Boots') 90 and *n*, 91, 103, 104 and *n*, 108 and *n*, 136, 142
Redgrave, William 90
Reeve, John 70, 74 and *n*, 76, 114*n*, 120 and *n*, 121, 122, 124
Reiss, Delia 90
Rie, Lucie 8*n*, 94*n*, 104 and *n*
Rockland State Mental Hospital 25
Rokkoyo (Six Old Kilns of Japan) 48
Roosevelt, Franklin 18
Rose, Muriel 94*n*
Rothschild, Henry 84, 110
Ruskin, John 10
sabi 11
Sainsbury Centre for the Arts 142
Schlanger, Jeff (with Takaezu, Toshiko) *Maija Grotell: Works Which Grow From Belief* 24*n*
Scott, Trudi 98, 130
Seibu Department Store 129
shibui 11, 42
Shields, Michael 112*n*
Shimpo wheel 114

Shin 30 and *n*
Shinto 52
Sidney, Jonathan *Janet Leach – New Pots* 82*n*, 116*n*
Southover Gallery 136
Steiner, Rudolf 10, 26 and *n*
Stichbury, Peter 74
St Ives Handicraft Guild 62*n*
Stocker, Norman 72*n*
Takaezu, Toshiko (with Schlanger, Jeff) *Maija Grotell: Works which Grow From Belief* 24*n*
Tate Gallery (St Ives) 140
Temple, Byron 74 and *n*, 123-124, 126
Texas Centennial Exposition, Dallas (1936) 16 and *n*
Threefold Farm (New York State) 5, 10, 25, 26-28, 34, 36, 56, 60, 93, 96
Tobey, Mark 58*n*, 96, 102*n*, 104*n*
Tomimoto, Kenkichi 47
Tomkins, Guy 112*n*
Tooby, Mike 140
Turino, Joe (first husband of JL) 20
Turnquist, Thomas *New York City Ceramics, Part 1, The Inwood Pottery Studios* 24*n*
Uchida, Yoshiko *To Learn Local Methods* 38*n*
University College of the Creative Arts, Farnham 132*n*
Vibert, Frank 68, 72
Victoria & Albert Museum 110 and *n*, 128, 129
Vincentelli, Moira *Women and Ceramics: Gendered Vessels* 8*n*
Voorhees, Aimee LePrince 24 and *n*
Voorhees, Harry 24
wabi 11
Wason, Jason 140
Wason, Joanna 140 and *n*, 142, 143
Webb, Aileen Osborn 110 and *n*
Welch, Robin 74
Wenford Bridge Pottery 76 and *n*
Wildenhain, Marguerite 28 and *n*, 30
Williams, Gerry *Janet Leach: American Foreigner* 10*n*, 20*n*, 24*n*, 26*n*, 30*n*, 32*n*, 36*n*, 92*n*, 132*n*
Wingfield Digby Collection 140
Wollands 84*n*
World Craft Council 110 and *n*
Yanagi, Soetsu 28, 30 and *n*, 32, 42, 44 and *n*, 56, 58 and *n*
Yates, Mary 100*n*, 103, 106 and *n*
Zen 11, 30, 42, 76, 83, 100